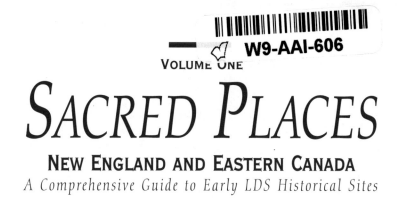

VOLUME ONE

# SACRED PLACES

## NEW ENGLAND AND EASTERN CANADA

*A Comprehensive Guide to Early LDS Historical Sites*

## Series Titles

NEW ENGLAND AND EASTERN CANADA

## Other Titles Planned for the Series

NEW YORK AND PENNSYLVANIA
OHIO AND ILLINOIS
MISSOURI
IOWA AND NEBRASKA
WYOMING AND UTAH

VOLUME ONE

# SACRED PLACES

## NEW ENGLAND AND EASTERN CANADA

*A Comprehensive Guide to Early LDS Historical Sites*

## LaMar C. Berrett,
*General Editor*

A. Gary Anderson
Donald Q. Cannon
Larry E. Dahl
Larry C. Porter

Bookcraft
Salt Lake City, Utah

Library of Congress Catalog Card Number 99-72525
ISBN 1-57008-644-3


First Printing, 1999


Printed in the United States of America

# CONTENTS

ॐ

# PREFACE

❧

When the Prophet Moses came to the mountain of God and the burning bush, the Lord said unto him, "Put off thy shoes from off thy feet, for the place whereon thou standest is holy ground" (Ex. 3:5).

Through the ages, the locations at which sacred historical events occurred have traditionally become holy. How holy or sacred a site is depends on the understanding of those beholding it. Elizabeth Barrett Browning wrote that "Earth's crammed with heaven / And every common bush afire with God; / But only he who sees, takes off his shoes—; / The rest sit around it and pluck blackberries" (*Aurora Leigh*, Book VII, II. 820–23).

The Church has a long tradition of recognizing and recording sacred places and events. In 1838 the Lord said to Joseph Smith, "Let the city, Far West, be a holy and consecrated land unto me; and it shall be called most holy, for the ground upon which thou standest is holy" (D&C 115:7). Even earlier, when the Church was organized on April 6, 1830, the Prophet was told that "there shall be a record kept among you" (D&C 21:1). Since those early times, places and events central to the Church's struggles and successes have been sanctified and recorded. *Sacred Places* endeavors to bring the history and geography of the early period of the Church to life.

Following the history and movement of the Saints from their early days in New York through to their settlement in the valley of the Great Salt Lake, this series will function as a valuable resource for academic historians and amateur Church history enthusiasts alike. *Sacred Places* provides detailed maps, interesting narratives, and numerous photographs in its effort to document the many places made sacred by the faith and testimonies of past generations of Saints. The comprehensive nature of the guide encourages readers to follow in the footsteps of Joseph Smith, Brigham Young, and other Church leaders, or to seek out the paths of their own ancestors. The series also enables armchair tourists to vicariously visit the many magnificent places relevant to Church history.

    *Sacred Places* is the culmination of over 25 years of research and study. Its authors, all university professors, have devoted much of their lives to this work—to the work of preserving and documenting the legacy of our literal and spiritual ancestors. By purchasing and preserving many of these sacred sites, modern prophets have encouraged member and nonmember alike to visit locations important to our history. Visiting sites such as the Sacred Grove, the Hill Cumorah, Adam-ondi-Ahman, or the Liberty and Carthage jails enables us to understand the history of the Church in terms of the real places and real people who witnessed the very real and sacred events of the Restoration.

# ACKNOWLEDGMENTS

So many individuals have contributed to the completion of *Sacred Places* that it is impractical, even impossible, to give personal credit to all those who deserve it. A blanket "Thank you" is given to all who have helped in any way.

Brigham Young University's College of Religious Instruction, Church History Department and Religious Studies Center have been instrumental in the realization of *Sacred Places*. Through various means—time, student assistants, secretarial help, research grants, and various other forms of financial aid—these organizations and the people associated with them have been indispensable.

Gratitude is expressed to the past and present General Authorities of The Church of Jesus Christ of Latter-day Saints who have ensured that significant Church history sites have been purchased and preserved for the edification and enjoyment of future generations. General editor LaMar C. Berrett is particularly grateful to President Spencer W. Kimball, who told him that, "We need to know and tell the truth about our Church history sites." President Kimball also related a fable to the editor concerning the Joseph Smith home in Palmyra, NY. "Some used to say that when the angel Moroni appeared to Joseph Smith the first time, it occurred in the Joseph Smith frame home," he stated, adding "but we know that this is not true." This statement has impressed upon the editor the great responsibility he has in providing accurate and correct information regarding our tremendous heritage and its relation to these sacred sites. *Sacred Places* has been significantly impacted by this great prophet's interest and encouragement. Special thanks are also given to those writers, researchers, journal keepers, Church historians, and others who laid the groundwork upon which *Sacred Places* has been constructed.

We are grateful to the staffs and administrators of the many repositories who have been so helpful in our research.

Especially gracious were the staffs of the Brigham Young University Harold B. Lee Library, Provo, UT, and the LDS Church Archives, Salt Lake City, UT. We are also grateful for the efforts of archaeologists Ray T. Matheny, Dale Berge, and Virginia Harrington in conducting archaeological digs at various Church history sites.

A special thanks is given to Wilford C. Wood who spent much of his life purchasing and preserving sites and objects pertaining to the life of the Prophet Joseph Smith.

We are grateful to the personnel at Bookcraft, Inc., who have helped bring this series to publication. We especially acknowledge Alan Ashton, Brad Pelo, Cory Maxwell, Dennis Madson, Jana Erickson, Cheryl Boyle, and Preston Draper for their efforts in editing and publishing this important information.

Finally we thank our wives and children for their patience and support over the past 25 years as we have labored to bring about this monumental work.

# INFORMATION CONTAINED
# IN *SACRED PLACES*
### ❧

Several symbols have been employed in *Sacred Places*. These symbols include small black squares ■ (both in text and on maps) indicating sites with direct ties to LDS history. Other important sites are denoted with small black circles ● to indicate that though they are not specifically related to LDS history they are nonetheless significant. $ Dollar signs have been placed near some of the descriptions of sites to indicate that these locations may charge an entrance fee. Please note that the use of the $ is not comprehensive, and that because of possible ownership or managerial changes at specific sites, fee information contained in the book may not be completely accurate.

Because of the voluminous nature of the information sources used by the authors, abbreviations were used in text to identify various sources. A complete alphabetic listing of abbreviations and their full bibliographies is included in the back of the volume. Also included is a list of abbreviations used to identify sources of photographs and other illustrations.

Many maps and other illustrations, including photographs, have been included in an effort to help the reader to locate, visualize, and more fully appreciate the numerous sites identified in *Sacred Places*.

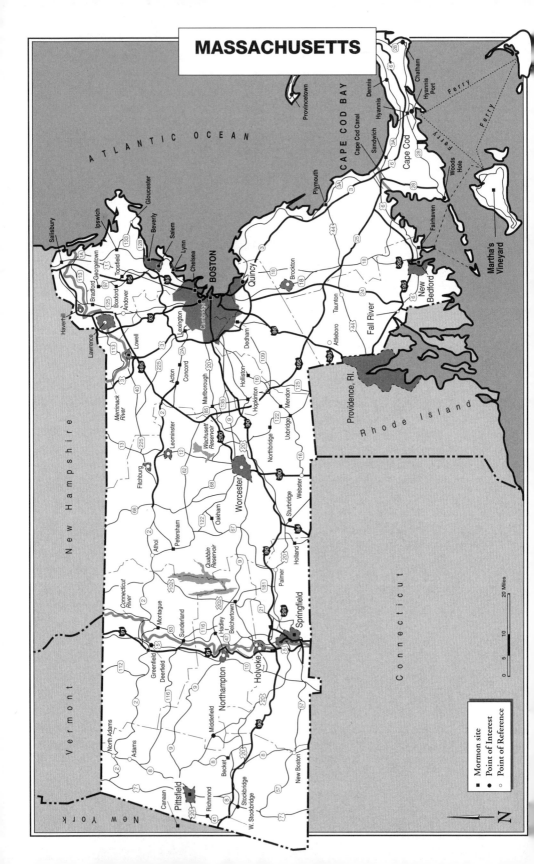

# MASSACHUSETTS

WITH SELECTED SITES IN CONNECTICUT AND RHODE ISLAND

## Donald Q. Cannon

ঌ

THE NEW ENGLAND STATE OF MASSACHUSETTS, nicknamed "the Bay State," takes its name from the Massachusetts Indian tribe. This tribe was part of the larger group of Native Americans who spoke the Algonquian language.

The first European visitor to what is now Massachusetts was the Venetian navigator John Cabot, who sailed from England in 1497. The earliest settlers came to Massachusetts for religious reasons, the Separatists settling Plymouth and the Puritans locating on the north shore of Massachusetts Bay.

The Commonwealth of Massachusetts, which developed under Puritan leadership, became an important force in the British colonies along the Atlantic seaboard. By the mid-18th century it played a key role in the events leading to the American Revolution. The first fighting in the American Revolution took place in Massachusetts. Lexington and Concord have become synonymous with the quest for freedom. Massachusetts contributed its share of heroes in the Revolution, and also many of the Founding Fathers hailed from the Bay State. In the War of 1812, Massachusetts again played a significant role.

The contribution of Massachusetts to the nation can be seen in the number of U.S. presidents from the state: John Adams, John Quincy Adams, Calvin Coolidge, and John F. Kennedy.

During the 19th century Massachusetts welcomed large numbers of immigrants. During this time industrialization in the form of factories also emerged. By the 20th century Massachusetts had become a populous state with a large variety of ethnic groups. By mid-century the factories of the 1800s were being replaced by high-technology industries, supported by some of the finest universities in the nation.

*1*

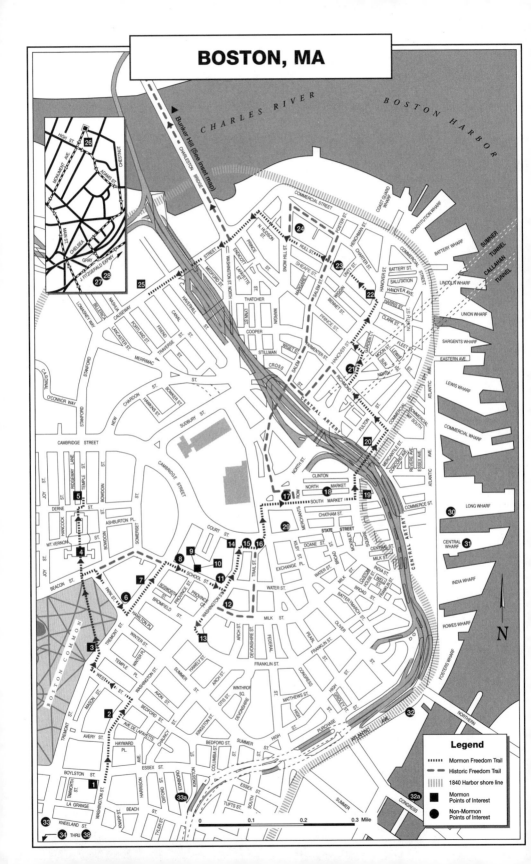

# BOSTON, MA

# Latter-day Saints in Massachusetts

The history of the LDS Church in Massachusetts has been peripheral to the mainstream of LDS history. However, many of the early leaders of the Church came from New England or had New England ancestry. After the Church was organized in New York, missionaries converted many New Englanders, who then gathered to the ever-relocating centers of the Church.

Since World War II, a fairly sizeable Church membership has emerged in Massachusetts. This growth has centered primarily around the state's many universities, especially Harvard. In addition to students, some LDS businessmen, engineers, and others have found work in Massachusetts, thus increasing Church membership.

## ■ Boston

**Samuel H. Smith,** one of the Prophet Joseph Smith's brothers, and **Orson Hyde** arrived in Boston June 22, 1832, becoming the first LDS missionaries to preach the restored gospel in Massachusetts. Four days after their arrival they baptized four persons. By the end of the year they had built up the **first branch** of the Church in Boston (EnH 211, 482; BiE 1:280).

The **Prophet Joseph Smith** and **Bishop Newel K. Whitney** were in Boston during Oct. 1832, on a very brief visit (HC 1:295).

**Members of the Twelve** preached in Boston in 1835 while on their first mission after being ordained Apostles (M&A v. 2, no. 1, p. 206). **Willard Richards** was practicing medicine near here when he saw the Book of Mormon for the first time in the summer of 1835. Brigham Young had left the book in Southborough (BiE 1:53). **Brigham Young** and his brother **Joseph** were among those who preached here in 1836. They eventually baptized 17 people (HC 2:466; EnH 482; HIB 153–56). **Joseph Smith** went from Providence, RI, to Boston by steam car on his way to Salem, where he arrived in Aug. 1836 (HC 2:463–64).

**Wilford Woodruff** held meetings in Boston in May 1838, and in 1841 **Erastus Snow** (Apostle 1849–88) and **George J. Adams** labored as missionaries in the area. A conference was held in Sept. 1841, eight members of the **Quorum of the Twelve** being in attendance. Political and spiritual preaching **conferences** were held in

Boston in July of 1844. Regular preaching meetings were held in Franklin Hall.

**Ezra T. Benson** met with **Col. Thomas L. Kane** in Boston on Feb. 12, 1848, to "discuss the possibilities of raising means from among the well-to-do non-members in the east to help the Saints who had been driven from their homes in Illinois" (MNE 220). The *Boston Post* reported on Feb. 16, 1848, that a meeting on the subject "of the suffering condition of the Mormons" had recently been held and was attended by prominent citizens. By Mar. 3, 1848, a subscription list was compiled to help the Mormons (MNE 221). **Wilford Woodruff** of the Twelve came to Boston in the spring of 1848 to gather the Saints in the New England states and lead them to the Rocky Mountains. He labored for two years until the spring of 1850 (ThC 10:147). One of the Saints who left Boston with his family on Apr. 19, 1850, was **Leonard Wilford Hardy,** who later served as first counselor to Presiding Bishop Edward Hunter from 1856 to 1883 (BiE 1:237).

### The Freedom Trail and LDS Church History Sites

The famous **Freedom Trail Walking Tour** is 1½ miles in length and includes most of the major colonial and Revolutionary historical sites in Boston. The trail is marked with a painted red line. A common starting point is the **information kiosk** on the east side of **Boston Common** across from West Street.

To include LDS **Historical Sites** along the Freedom Trail, the starting point would be the **Boylston Hall** site at the corner of Boylston and Washington Streets, one block east of the SE corner of the Boston Common. Including the LDS sites adds about ½ mile to the tour. In the text below, sites that are LDS-related are identified with a ■.

■ **1. BOYLSTON HALL.** This building was used for Church **conferences** and **Mormon missionary preaching meetings** held in Boston during Feb., Mar., and Sept. 1843. The hall was on the third floor of the Boylston Market Building, which was located on the SW corner where Boylston Street connects with Washington Street. The building was built of brick in 1809 at a cost of $59,560. The first floor had twelve stalls for markets, the second floor had four large rooms, and the third floor had an organ in a "spacious" 50' x 100' hall designed for large meetings. The original building was destroyed in 1888.

In Feb. 1843, 14 branches comprising 793 members were represented at two conferences held in Boylston Hall (HC 5:268; EnH 212). A September conference was presided over by eight members of the **Quorum of the Twelve** (HC 6:11–30; WW 192–93).

Mormon missionary preaching meetings were held several times in Boylston Hall during Mar. 1843. Crowds of up to 500 people, including legislators and other prominent people, were addressed by Elder **George J. Adams.** A very favorable report of these meetings was printed in *The Boston Weekly Bee* newspaper Apr. 1, 1843 (HC 5:322–23; EnH 212).

*Boylston Hall and Market, Boston, 1809. (Courtesy of Houghton Mifflin Co.)*

After receiving knowledge of Joseph Smith's martyrdom, a **meeting** was held in a **hall** on Washington Street opposite Boylston Hall on July 18, 1844. **Brigham Young** and the other speakers spoke on **The Martyrdom and Its Effects.** The Twelve published a comforting epistle to the Saints in the *Prophet* on this same day (HC 7:198–99). Two days after the meeting, the **Twelve** left for Nauvoo (WW 209).

While in the city of Boston, **Wilford Woodruff** had a **vision** of "going to the Rocky Mountains to build a Temple there and to dedicate it to the Lord" (WW 584).

■ **2. THE MELODEON HALL AND JOSEPH SMITH FOR PRESIDENT.** The Melodeon was a small public theater hall located at 545–47 Washington Street (No. 361 in 1844) between the Paramount Theatre on the south and the Opera House on the north. Now it is directly at the west end of Avenue De LaFayette. The hall was built in 1835 and went through many changes. In 1894 the showy B.F. Keith New Theatre, with its glass staircase over a waterfall, made the vaudeville theatre an important showplace. The Melodeon Hall was the scene of a **state convention** held July 1, 1844, with Brigham Young presiding. The Twelve and the other missionaries present were campaigning for Joseph Smith as a candidate for the presidency of the United States. In the evening session there were so many "rowdies" present that the police couldn't control them and the meeting was broken up. During the meetings earlier in the day, **Joseph Smith** and **Sidney Rigdon** had been **nominated for president and vice president of the United States,** respectively. The Twelve did not know that Joseph

*Melodeon Hall, 545-547 So. Washington St., Boston. The building is between the Paramount Theatre on the left and the Opera House on the right. (1985)*

Smith had been martyred five days earlier. Proceedings of the convention were published in the *Boston Times* on July 2, 1844 (MNE 192–93; WW 206–7). A day later Heber C. Kimball and George B. Wallace were elected delegates to attend the Baltimore National Convention on July 13 (WW 207).

■ **3. BOSTON COMMON (1634).** The oldest public park in the country is a 48-acre "common" that was first used as a pasture and militia training ground. The Puritans also kept stocks here for punishment of those who profaned the Sabbath. It was here the British prepared for the Battle of Bunker Hill.

After **John C. Bennett's** excommunication from the LDS Church, and while living in Plymouth, MA, he organized the first poultry show in America—it was held on the Boston Common.

On July 4, 1844, **Brigham Young, Heber C. Kimball,** and others of the Twelve watched fireworks on the Common (HC 7:168). They were in Boston for conferences, both spiritual and political.

An **information kiosk** is located on the east side of Boston Common across from West Street.

■ **4. MASSACHUSETTS STATE HOUSE AND ARCHIVES (1795).** The gold-dome State House is located on the top of Beacon Hill at the NW corner of Boston Common. Today it houses statues, historic paintings, flags, war relics, and original documents such as the charter of the Massachusetts Bay Company. In front of the State House is a statue of so-called religious heretic Anne Hutchinson (1591–1643) sculptured by Cyrus E. Dallin, who was raised in Springville, Utah. **Brigham Young** visited the State House Sept. 22, 1843, while on a mission to the East.

A walk along Beacon Street and the area west of the State House takes you past shuttered brick townhouses where many of Boston's wealthy and socially prominent families lived during the 19th century.

■ **5. HOME OF SISTER VOSE.** A home once found behind the State House at 57 Temple Street (located about where the entrance to the Suffolk University Law School auditorium is) was the scene of a very touching and sad event in the lives of two members of the Quorum of the Twelve: **Wilford Woodruff** and **Brigham Young.** On July 17, 1844, the Quorum of Twelve gathered in Boston. From here they were to return to Nauvoo in response to the deaths of the Prophet Joseph Smith and his brother Hyrum. The Twelve were to travel under the direction of Brigham Young, senior member of the Quorum. Wilford Woodruff described the sadness of that day in his journal: "Elder Brigham Young arrived in Boston. I walked with him to No. 57 Temple Street and called upon Sister Vose. Brother Young took the bed and I the armchair, and then we veiled our faces and gave vent to our grief" (WW 208; HC 7:195). On July 23, Brigham Young and members of the Twelve left Boston on their sorrowful journey to Nauvoo (ThP v. 1, no. 11, p. 2).

● **6. PARK STREET CHURCH (1809).** Located on the NE corner of the Boston Common and on the north corner of Park and Tremont Streets is the Park Street Church, which was used as a store for brimstone (sulphur) during the War of 1812. The corner was known as "Brimstone Corner." The church was the scene of **William Lloyd Garrison's** famous anti-slavery address of July 4, 1829. On the same day three years later, the song **"America"** was sung in the church for the first time publicly.

■ **7. GRANARY BURYING GROUND.** Located just north of the Park Street Church on Tremont Street, the Granary Burying Ground is the burial site of three signers of the Declaration of Independence:

John Hancock, Samuel Adams, and Robert T. Payne. All of these men called upon Wilford Woodruff in the St. George Temple and "demanded" that the ordinances of the temple be performed for them. Their temple work was done shortly thereafter (TMH 90–91). Paul Revere, Peter Faneuil, Ben Franklin's parents, and victims of the Boston Massacre are also buried here.

● **8. KING'S CHAPEL (1754).** On the NE corner of Tremont and School Streets stands the first Anglican Church in Boston. During British rule it was favored with gifts of silver and vestments by Queen Anne and George III. After the Revolution it became America's first Unitarian Church. **John Winthrop,** founder of Boston, is buried in the cemetery next door. On the opposite corner (south) is the **Parker House,** the hotel that gave its name to Parker House Rolls.

■ **9. OLD BOSTON CITY HALL, FIRST PUBLIC SCHOOL SITE, AND BEN FRANKLIN AND MAYOR JOSIAH QUINCY STATUES.** Located on the left as one turns right on School Street is the **Old Boston City Hall.** A **schoolhouse** built in 1635 once occupied this site. It became a public Latin school and the **first public school in America.** Rev. Cotton Mather, John Hancock, Ralph Waldo Emerson, and Samuel Adams were students here. On the left as one faces City Hall is an 1856 statue of **Benjamin Franklin.** There is also an 1879 statue of **Josiah Quincy** (1772–1864), who was mayor of Boston 1823–28 and president of Harvard 1829–46.

**Josiah Quincy** (1802–82), son of the Josiah Quincy whose statue is located here, was also the mayor of Boston from 1845 to 1849. The younger Josiah, with his cousin Charles Francis Adams, son of John Quincy Adams, visited **Joseph Smith** at the Mansion House in Nauvoo on May 15, 1844. Joseph autographed a *Book of Mormon* Quincy had purchased (owned now by the LDS Church). Quincy later published a book in Boston titled *Figures of the Past* (1883). He devoted the last chapter, "Joseph Smith at Nauvoo," to the Prophet. Although Quincy's evaluation of Joseph Smith is skeptical, he did make many statements that were both complimentary and "prophetic":

> It is by no means improbable that some future text-book, for the use of generations yet unborn, will contain a question something like this: What historical American of the nine-

teenth century has exerted the most powerful influence upon the destinies of his countrymen? And it is by no means impossible that the answer to that interrogatory may be thus written: *Joseph Smith, the Mormon prophet.* And the reply, absurd as it doubtless seems to most men now living, may be an obvious commonplace to their descendants. History deals in surprises and paradoxes quite as startling as this. The man who established a religion in this age of free debate, who was and is today accepted by hundreds of thousands as a direct emissary from the Most High,—such a rare human being is not to be disposed of by pelting his memory with unsavory epithets. Fanatic, impostor, charlatan, he may have been; but these hard names furnish no solution to the problem he presents to us. Fanatics and impostors are living and dying every day, and their memory is buried with them; but the wonderful influence which this founder of a religion exerted and still exerts throws him into relief before us, not as a rogue to be criminated, but as a phenomenon to be explained (FOP 376–77).

■ **10. "OLD OLD" COUNTY COURT HOUSE SITE.** The "Old Old" County Court House was located where the present "Old" City Hall stands. The "Old Old" County Court House was remodelled in 1840 as the "Old" City Hall. A "New Old" County Court House was built in 1836 just behind (north of) the present City Hall. The "Old Old" County Court House had a cupola from which one could view the city.

In May 1838, **Wilford Woodruff** spent several days in Boston holding meetings with the Saints. On May 11, he visited **Bunker Hill Monument.** He then viewed the city of Boston from the **"Old Old" County Court House Cupola** before visiting the Saints in Cambridge (WW 89–90).

● **11. OLD CORNER BOOKSTORE (1712).** Located on the NW corner of School and Washington Streets, this building was a publishing house and later a bookstore. It was a meeting place of literary greats: Emerson, Hawthorne, Holmes, Thoreau, Stowe, and others. The bookstore is now a store and museum.

● **12. OLD SOUTH MEETING HOUSE (1729).** Located just south of the Old Corner Bookstore on the east side of Washington Street and on the corner of Milk Street, this structure was built as the third

Congregational Church in Boston. It was the major large meeting house of colonial days. When Boston's town meetings became too large for Faneuil Hall, the colonists met here. Many mass meetings were held here in preparation for the Revolutionary War. Planning meetings for the Boston Tea Party were held here and from here the "Party" was launched. Citizens went east along Milk Street, then east on Congress Street to the tea party ship *Beaver.* Just behind the church and across Milk Street on the south side is the **birthplace of Ben Franklin.**

■   **13. FRANKLIN HALL SITE.** Franklin Hall was located at 16 Franklin Street. The location today is in the center of a small triangular park with trees and brick pavement. It is named Lincoln Filene Park after civic leader and merchant Lincoln Filene (1865–1957), who presented the park to the city. The area is also called "Downtown Crossing." Franklin Hall was located about 100 feet southeast of Washington Street on the northeast side of Franklin Street, which in the 1800s ran parallel to and near the northeast side of Filene's Department Store. Franklin Hall was opposite and centered on Filene's.

   **Franklin Hall** was the usual weekly **Sabbath meeting place** of the Saints living in the Boston area in 1844. **The Twelve** held a **conference** there with the Saints on June 29–30, and July 2, 1844. Those present were Brigham Young, Heber C. Kimball, Orson Hyde, Orson Pratt, Wilford Woodruff, William Smith, and Lyman Wight. Both gospel and political topics were discussed (HC 7:149, 159; WW 206–7).

■   **14. LELAND AND WHITING PUBLISHING CO.** Located at 71 Washington Street was the publisher of a bitter anti-Mormon book in 1842 titled *The History of the Saints; or An Exposé of Joe Smith and Mormonism.* The author of the book was **John C. Bennett,** ex-Mormon and former mayor of Nauvoo. (The Boston Co. building, located opposite the Old State House to the west, covers the No. 71 site at its NE corner, which is directly west of the west end of State Street.)

   The **first anti-Mormon pamphlet,** written by Rev. Alexander Campbell, one of the founders of the "Disciples," or Campbellites, had been published in 1832 at another site by publisher Benjamin H. Greene of Boston under the title of *Delusions: An Analysis of the Book of Mormon.* It was a 16-page reprint of Campbell's article that was originally published in the *Millennial Harbinger.* Joseph Smith denounced the pamphlet (HC 2:268–70).

$ ● **15. OLD STATE HOUSE (1712).** The Old State House was called the Town House (1657) before the Revolution. It is located a long block north of the Old Corner Bookstore on the east side of Washington Street with one side facing State Street. This was the Massachusetts provincial government headquarters during colonial days. Here John Hancock and Samuel Adams denounced the tax laws of Parliament. This was the first state capitol of Massachusetts. The Declaration of Independence was read for the first time in Boston from its eastern balcony on July 18, 1776. The building now houses the Museum of Boston History.

On the south side of State Street at No. 15, opposite the Old State House, is the **Boston National Historical Park Visitor Center** with restrooms and information.

● **16. BOSTON MASSACRE SITE (Mar. 5, 1770).** Sixty feet into the intersection east of the Old State House is a circle of cobblestones within a curbed triangle. The cobblestones mark the site where a British guard of nine soldiers clashed with an unruly mob. Five colonists were killed.

● **17. FANEUIL HALL (1742, rebuilt in 1761 and 1806).** Faneuil (pronounced *Fan'l*) Hall is located a block north and half a block east of the Old State House. It is one of the most famous meeting places in the world. It was built in 1742 by Peter Faneuil and then was given to the city. Town meetings in the upper hall were so active here that John Adams called it the "Cradle of Liberty." It houses a public market on the bottom floor, a meeting hall on the second floor, and a military museum on the third floor. A **statue of Samuel Adams** is located in front of the hall.

● **18. FANEUIL HALL MARKETPLACE.** The marketplace is located east of Faneuil Hall. It consists of three 500-foot long buildings conceived by Mayor Josiah Quincy and first opened Aug. 26, 1826. In those days Boston's waterfront was very near the east doors of the buildings, and boats docked here to sell their wares. Today the buildings are lined with stores, shops, and restaurants. It also boasts the largest open-air fruit and vegetable market in the U.S. Beyond is the waterfront of Boston Harbor, one of the oldest ports in America.

■  **19. BOSTON HARBOR.** Located at the mouth of the Charles River on Boston Bay was the old Boston Harbor—the port of entry to the U.S. for many Saints. Some of the old harbor has been filled in, but in earlier days the whole northeast end of Boston was a mass of wharves for docking ships. Commercial Wharf and Long Wharf (1710) were central among all the wharves, extending into the bay from the present-day Commercial Street near the east end of the present Faneuil Hall Marketplace. Commercial Street separated the buildings of the market from the waters of the harbor.

In 1638 **Robert Smith,** Joseph Smith's great-great-great-grandfather, sailed from Boston, England, and arrived at **Boston Harbor** in May, at about age fourteen. He lived in Boston and worked as a tailor. It is said that he built Boston's third house that had a cellar in it (LAP 20–24).

In 1630, **John Mack,** Joseph Smith's great-great-grandfather sailed from Scotland and arrived at **Boston Harbor** at about age eighteen.

In 1856–57, **Handcart Saints** must have had feelings of gratitude as they sighted the Boston Harbor after spending five or six weeks in the hold of a sailing vessel. At least 3060 emigrating Saints who boarded ships in Liverpool, England, arrived in Boston in 1856–57. About 2040 of them became participants in the famous pioneer companies that pushed handcarts some 1400 miles from Iowa City, Iowa to Salt Lake City. They traveled by train from Boston to Iowa City via New York City. Two-thirds of the 2962 handcart company participants sailed into the Boston Harbor on the ships *Enoch Train, S. Curling, Horizon, Wellfleet,* and *George Washington.* The Edward Martin handcart company came on the *Horizon* (HTZ; EnH 482).

■  **20. ABIJAH TEWKESBURY'S SHIPPING OFFICE AND MORMON MEETING HOUSE.** These were located in a brick building not far from Faneuil Hall at **82 Commercial Street.** To locate the shipping office, go east from Faneuil Hall through the Marketplace. Commercial Street is located near the east end of the market. Go north (left) on Commercial Street. Continue under the elevated U.S. 1. A third of a block past U.S. 1 and on the left side (NW) is No. 82, the former shipping office.

Abijah Tewkesbury was the first convert of Freeman Nickerson who labored as a missionary in Boston during the years 1841–42. In Mar. 1842 with thirty converts, the **Boston Branch** was **Reorga-**

**nized** in Tewkesbury's Shipping Office, and Church meetings continued to be held here (ENS Nov. 1973, pp. 17–19).

$ ● **21. PAUL REVERE HOUSE (1676).** The Paul Revere House is located NE of Faneuil Hall, north of the elevated John F. Fitzgerald Expressway, on North Street. This is the oldest frame dwelling in Boston. Revere owned it from 1770–1800. He left this house to partic-

*Abijah Tewkesbury's Shipping Office, 82 Commercial St., Boston. Identified by the eleventh window from the left. (1985)*

ipate in the Boston Tea Party (1773) and to make his historic April 18, 1775, ride to Lexington and Concord.

■ **22. PAUL REVERE MALL AND STATUE.** These sites are located across Hanover Street from St. Stephen's Church (the only surviving Bullfinch Church in Boston) and just east of the Old North Church.

The equestrian statue of Paul Revere is the work of Utah-born Cyrus E. Dallin, who considered this statue his masterpiece. He started this art project at age twenty-two and it took fifty-seven years and seven models before the City of Boston would erect the statue in 1940. Cyrus E. Dallin was born in 1861 and named after Cyrus Wheelock, who had converted his father to Mormonism. His parents settled in Springville, Utah. Cyrus was never baptized into the Church. At age eighteen he moved to Boston to study sculpture. He lived in Boston most of his life and taught at the Massachusetts Normal School of Art. Cyrus Dallin also sculptured *Angel Moroni* for the Salt Lake Temple, the *Brigham Young Monument* in the center of Main Street in Salt Lake City, and *Massasoit* at Plymouth (UHQ v. 44, no. 1, pp. 4–39).

● **23. OLD NORTH CHURCH, OR CHRIST CHURCH (1723).** Located on Salem Street near Tileson Street, this church was a place of worship for non-Puritan Anglicans. It is the city's oldest standing church still in use.

On Apr. 18, 1775, the sexton Robert Newman (and perhaps a man named John Pulling) hung two lanterns in the belfry of the steeple which signalled the **patriots** across the Charles River that the British were leaving Boston on their way to Lexington and Concord "by sea." It was at this time also that **Paul Revere** started on his famous ride. In 1781 the bells in the steeple rang out at the good news that Cornwallis had surrendered at Yorktown.

● **24. COPP'S HILL BURYING GROUND (1660).** Boston's second cemetery is located just up the hill from the Old North Church. Here the British aimed their cannon at Charlestown and Bunker Hill.

■ **25. OLD NORTH RAILROAD STATION AND THE MARTYRDOM.** Located in the NE corner of Boston on Causeway Street, which runs SW from the end of Commercial Street, is the Old North Railroad Station.

On June 27, 1844, the day of the **Prophet Joseph Smith's Martyrdom, Orson Hyde,** an Apostle, was laboring as a missionary in Boston. On that fateful day Orson felt a heavy depression of mind. **Brigham Young** and **Wilford Woodruff** also had a similar experience as they sat in the **Old North Railroad Station** waiting for a train to Salem. This experience happened at the very hour of the Martyrdom. Brigham Young said he had "a heavy depression of spirit, and so melancholy I could not converse with any degree of pleasure" (MS 26:343; HC 7:132; WW 206).

■ **26. BUNKER HILL MONUMENT.** The monument is located across the Charles River on Breed's Hill, where the battle actually took place. It is south of the real Bunker's Hill. On top of Breed's Hill is a 221-foot high granite obelisk commemorating the first major battle of the Revolution (June 17, 1775). The monument gives tribute to the colonists who withdrew and rallied to organize an American army.

One of the American soldiers that participated in the Battle of Bunker's Hill was **William Duty,** brother of Mary Duty (Asael Smith's wife and Joseph Smith's grandmother).

On Sept. 22, 1843, **Brigham Young** visited Bunker Hill while on a mission in the area.

On July 2, 1844, members of the **Quorum of the Twelve** held a political meeting here. They had already nominated Joseph Smith as a candidate for president of the United States in a meeting held July 1st in the Melodeon. In the July 2nd meeting, held at the monument at 4:00 P.M., **Heber C. Kimball** and **George B. Wallace** were elected delegates to attend the Baltimore National Convention to be held July 13, 1844. **Colonel Lyman Wight** then delivered a political address (HC 7:159; WW 207).

A grand view of the surrounding landscape can be had by climbing the spiral staircase to the top.

$ • **27. BUNKER HILL PAVILION.** Near U.S. 1 and one block SW of the USS *Constitution* at 55 Constitution Road in Charlestown, Bunker Hill Pavilion houses a multi-media presentation of the Battle of Bunker Hill titled **"Whites of Their Eyes."**

$ • **28. USS *CONSTITUTION* ("OLD IRONSIDES") (1797).** This rebuilt (15% original) oak 44-gun frigate located in the Charlestown Naval Yard is the oldest commissioned ship afloat in the world. Participating in 40 engagements against the French privateers in the 1790s and the British in the War of 1812, Old Ironsides was never defeated. The **USS *Constitution* Museum** is nearby.

### Beyond the Freedom Trail

$ • **29. "WHERE'S BOSTON?" SHOW AND EXHIBIT.** Located at 60 State Street, south of Faneuil Hall, this exhibit is a multi-image portrait of Boston with 3,100 slides and quadrophonic sound.

$ • **30. BOSTON HARBOR CRUISE.** Boats depart hourly from 11 A.M. to 4 P.M., with a sunset cruise at 7 P.M. (times may vary). The boats leave from 1 Long Wharf at the east end of State Street, just south of the Marriott Hotel.

$ • **31. NEW ENGLAND AQUARIUM.** Located on Central Wharf, the Aquarium exhibits 2,000 species of aquatic life from all seven seas.

• **32. THE TEA PARTY SITE.** The site is located on Atlantic Ave. about two blocks NE of Congress Street. The **Boston Tea Party Ship and Museum** (32a) is a full-size working replica of one of the original tea party ships and is located SE at the Congress Street Bridge.

• **33. THEATRE DISTRICT AND CHINATOWN.** These are located near the Boston Common. The **theatres** are located a block or two south of the SE corner of the Boston Common, and **Chinatown** (33a) is located about three blocks east of the same corner.

$ ●   **34. JOHN HANCOCK OBSERVATORY.** Located at Copley Square, this is "the best place to see Boston." It is 740 feet high, the tallest building in New England.

$ ●   **35. PRUDENTIAL CENTER.** Located in the Back Bay area of Boston, SW of the Common between Boylston Street and Huntington Ave., the Prudential Center has an enclosed shopping area within the 52-story Prudential Tower and the **Skywalk Observatory.**

●   **36. SYMPHONY HALL.** On the corner of Massachusetts and Huntington Avenues is the 2,600-seat Symphony Hall, home of the world-famous **Boston Symphony Orchestra** (founded in 1881) and the **Boston Pops Orchestra.** The season runs September through April.

●   **37. FENWAY PARK.** West of the Prudential Center is Fenway Park, the home of the Boston Red Sox baseball team. Their season runs from mid-April to early October.

$ ●   **38. JOHN F. KENNEDY LIBRARY.** At Columbia Point on Dorchester Bay is the John F. Kennedy Library, complete with films and exhibits about the famous president.

## Northwest of Boston

■   CAMBRIDGE

In 1630 Gov. John Winthrop founded New Towne, now called Cambridge, to be a place of protection from King Charles's warships. It is located west of Boston across the Charles River on State 2A.

The General Court of the Massachusetts Bay Colony agreed to give £400 toward a college in Oct. 1636. John Harvard, a young minister who was interested in higher education, died and left his estate of £1,700 and his library to the proposed college. The new college, named after Harvard, was founded in 1636, becoming the first university in what would be the United States. Cambridge is also the home of Radcliffe University and the Massachusetts Institute of Technology.

During the Revolutionary War, Cambridge was a vital center for the new nation. Here George Washington took command of the American army as commander-in-chief. **Longfellow's home,** a house which was used by Washington as his headquarters in 1775, is located at 105 Brattle St., across the street from the **Cambridge LDS chapel** and near the old LDS New England States Mission Home. Henry Wadsworth Longfellow, a young Harvard instructor, bought the home in 1843 and lived there until his death in 1882 (open to the public).

**Wilford Woodruff** visited fellow Saint A. P. Rockwood on May 11, 1832, at Cambridgeport. Rockwood was in jail because of a charge of debt. The jail term served also to trouble and distress Rockwood because of his Mormonism (WW 89–90).

● LEXINGTON—"**Birthplace of American Liberty**"

Eleven miles NW of Boston on State 4 is the famous **Battle Green** where the "first" battle of the Revolutionary War was fought on Apr. 19, 1775. The night before, Paul Revere rode his horse to Lexington via Arlington to warn the colonists that the British were on their way to Concord to destroy their military stores. Samuel Adams and John Hancock were sleeping in the **Hancock-Clarke House** (1698) when aroused by Revere on the night of Apr. 18, 1775. (To follow the Paul Revere route to Lexington from Harvard,

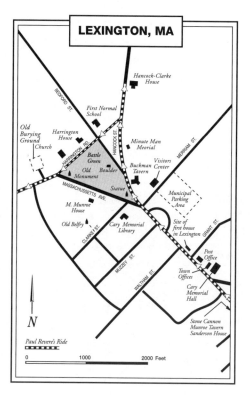

proceed from Harvard Square and follow Massachusetts Ave. through Arlington and on into Concord.)

The Lexington minute men under Captain Parker gathered on the green early in the morning and made **Buckman Tavern,** just northeast of the green, their headquarters. The **Munroe Tavern,** southeast on Massachusetts Ave., was the British headquarters.

Four hundred British soldiers under Major Pitcairn approached from the southeast. The site is marked today by a **Minute Man statue** facing the line of approach of the British.

The battle line of the 75 minute men is marked by a **boulder** on the northeast side of the Battle Green and the **"old monument"** on the west side of the green.

As the two military groups faced each other Pitcairn ordered the minute men to lay down their arms. No one obeyed. Parker's famous words pierced the morning air: "Stand your ground, don't fire unless fired upon, but if they mean to have a war let it begin here."

The engagement lasted only a few minutes. Eight minute men were killed. The British then marched on to Concord, where they successfully destroyed a large quantity of military stores. Seven of the eight minute men killed are buried under the **"old monument,"** the first Revolutionary monument publicly erected in the U.S. (1799).

●  MINUTE MAN NATIONAL HISTORICAL PARK AND BATTLE ROAD VISITOR CENTER

To get to Concord from Lexington one can travel over the route of Paul Revere's famous ride by going west on Massachusetts Ave., which turns into State 2A on the west side of Highway 128 (Boston's belt route). About ³⁄₄ mile west of State 128 is the **Battle Road Visitor Center.** It is located on the east end of the **Minute Man National Historical Park.** By following State 2A and Lexington Road you travel the basic route of Revere's ride.

■  CONCORD—Home of Joseph and Emma Smith's Ancestors

Concord is located 7 miles west of Lexington on State 2A (an extension of Massachusetts Ave.). It was incorporated in 1635 and is rich in history. It was here that the early patriots faced the British military at Old North Bridge and fired "the shot heard round the world."

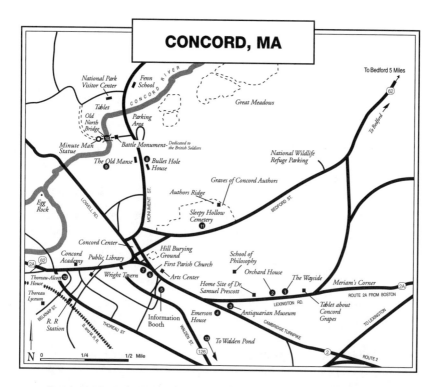

During the 1800s it became famous as the home of noted American authors Ralph Waldo Emerson, Nathaniel Hawthorne, Margaret Sidney, Louisa May Alcott, and Henry David Thoreau.

**John Heald,** ancestor of Emma Hale, Joseph Smith's wife, was one of the first settlers in Concord in 1635.

**John Mack,** Joseph Smith's great-great-grandfather, moved to Concord from Salisbury with his wife and first child. From here they moved to Lyme, CT (1734). **Samuel Smith II,** Joseph Smith's great-grandfather, served here as a delegate in the Provincial Congress (1774–75).

When entering Concord from the east on State 2A (Lexington Road), the following important historical sites may be visited in order of appearance:

- **1. THE WAYSIDE.** On the north side of Lexington Road in the outskirts of Concord is the home of the **Alcotts, Hawthorne,** and **Margaret Sidney.** Just east of the home is a tablet telling about the origin of the **Concord grape.**

$ ● **2. THE ORCHARD HOUSE.** Also on the north side of Lexington

Road, a little west of the Wayside, is the home of the **Alcotts** from 1858–77. It is the house described in *Little Women*.

$ ● **3. THE ANTIQUARIAN MUSEUM.** Located at 200 Lexington Road on the corner where Lexington Road meets the Cambridge Turnpike is the Antiquarian Museum. It contains battle relics, Emerson's study, Thoreau's cabin furniture, and one of **Paul Revere's lanterns.** Paul Revere was captured by the British as he made his way to Concord from Lexington. A **diorama** portrays the battle at the Old North Bridge.

$ ● **4. THE EMERSON HOUSE.** Located across the street SW of the Antiquarian Museum on the south side of the Cambridge Turnpike is the Emerson House. It was built in 1828 and was owned by Ralph Waldo Emerson from 1835 to 1882.

● **5. INFORMATION BOOTH.** The booth is located on a street going south from the Cambridge Turnpike just before the city center.

● **6. THE FIRST PARISH CHURCH.** This church is located on the south side of the street in the center of Concord. It was the site of the First Provincial Congress presided over by John Hancock.

● **7. THE WRIGHT TAVERN.** Located just west of the First Parish Church on the same side of the street, the tavern was built in 1747 and was the headquarters of the British commanders on Apr. 19, 1775.

● **8. BULLET HOLE HOUSE.** This house is located on the east side of Monument Street about two to three blocks north of the Concord city center. This is where Elisha Jones stored supplies for the minute men.

$ ● **9. THE OLD MANSE.** The home where **Emerson** and **Hawthorne** lived and wrote many of their early works is located on the west side of Monument Street just past Bullet Hole House.

● **10. OLD NORTH BRIDGE.** The bridge is a part of the Minute Man National Historical Park. The **Minute Man statue** by Daniel Chester French is located on the west side of the Concord River and the obelisk **battle monument** is located on the east side of the river. Both mark the respective locations of the minute men and the British soldiers when the first shot of the first "real" Revolutionary battle was fired and "heard round the world." D. C. French was the sculptor responsible for the Abra-

*Old North Bridge, Salem, MA. (1983)*

ham Lincoln National Monument at the end of the Mall in Washington D.C. **The National Park Service Visitor Center** is located in the old Buttrick Mansion above the battlefield.

- **11. SLEEPY HOLLOW CEMETERY.** About two blocks NE of the city center, Sleepy Hollow Cemetery has graves of Concord authors on **Authors Ridge** (north side). Thoreau, Emerson, Hawthorne, the Alcotts, and Ephraim Bull are all buried here.

- **12. THOREAU-ALCOTT HOUSE AND THOREAU LYCEUM.** These sites are located about three blocks SE of the city center. A reproduction of Thoreau's **Walden cabin** is located at the lyceum.

- **13. WALDEN POND AND THOREAU'S CABIN SITE.** Walden Pond and the cabin site are located on Walden Street (State 126) about a mile SE of the Concord city center.

- **ACTON—Birthplace of Thomas B. Marsh**

Twenty miles NW of Boston where State 27 crosses U.S. 2 is Acton, Middlesex Co., where Thomas B. Marsh was born on Nov. 1, 1800. He was ordained a member of the first Quorum of Twelve Apostles Apr. 26, 1835, and became the "senior member," or President of the Twelve, because of his seniority of age. Later it was determined his real birthday was in 1800 and not 1799. He would have been second in rank in the quorum had this been known. He was appointed President of the Church in Missouri pro tem Feb. 10, 1838; but in Aug. 1838, he became disaffected with the Church.

He was excommunicated Mar. 17, 1839. After eighteen years he was rebaptized in 1857 at Florence, NE, and moved to Utah that same year. He died a few years later in Ogden, UT (BiE 1:74–76; MAR).

■ LOWELL

Twenty-five miles NW of downtown Boston and just east of U.S. 3 is Lowell. **Orson Hyde** preached the gospel here in 1832. **Ezra T. Benson** and Jeremiah Willey preached here from Apr. to the fall of 1843. They organized a branch, with Elder Benson presiding.

    **Lucy Meserve Smith,** wife of George A. Smith, worked in a cotton factory in Lowell as a young woman in order to earn money to gather with the Saints in Nauvoo. She was born in Newry, ME, but after her baptism in 1837 moved to Lowell. While in Nauvoo she hired out as a weaver and spinner and was hired by Emma Smith, the Prophet Joseph's wife. At age 27 she became the second wife of George A. Smith (WV 261–71).

## North of Boston

■ CHELSEA

Two and a half miles north of the Boston Common on the Northeast Expressway is Chelsea, where **Erastus Snow,** Apostle from 1849 to 1888, served a mission from 1841 to 1843. During this time a Sister Spooner, who had been declared incurable, was healed of dropsy by the laying on of hands of Elder Snow (BiE 1:108).

■ LYNN

Nine miles NE of Boston Common on State 1A is the city of Lynn. In 1832 Elders **Orson Hyde** and **Samuel Smith,** brother of Joseph Smith, baptized several people here while on a mission to the eastern country. They tracted from house to house and preached to an overflow crowd in the **town hall** (BiE 1:280).

■ SALEM

Salem, located on the seacoast 15 miles NE of Boston on State 1A

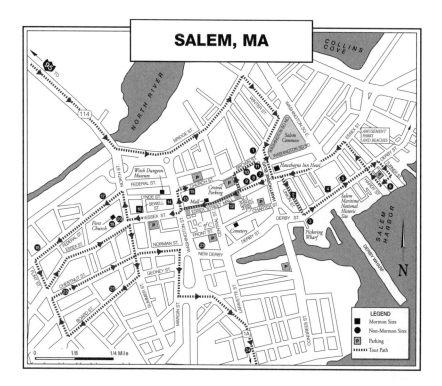

(Exit 25 E. off State 128), began as a fishing colony in 1626. It also became a trading station and missionary outpost. A corporation was formed to raise funds for the colony and was reorganized in 1629 with a royal charter. It was called the Massachusetts Bay Company. The town was named Salem from the Hebrew word *Shalom,* which means "peace."

In 1692 a group of young white girls who had been frightened by a slave's voodoo stories eventually accused the slave and two other unpopular women of witchcraft. Before this "epidemic" ended, over 200 people were accused of witchcraft in Salem and neighboring towns. Nineteen people were hung, several died in jail, and one was pressed to death. Gov. William Phipps and Increase Mather were instrumental in stopping the trials. All participants eventually expressed repentance over the matter.

Early citizens of Salem and other New England colonies believed in religious freedom as it applied only to themselves. Roger Williams was considered a troublemaker and was banished from Salem when he persisted in declaring that church and state should remain separate.

Salem architecture reflects the development of the entire

colonial period in New England and even today retains its colonial character.

Visitors to Salem are advised to park their cars and walk. A city tour by trolley leaves hourly (10 A.M.–5 P.M.) from Riley parking plaza.

### Latter-day Saints in Salem

Joseph Smith's grandfather **Solomon Mack** was a sailor who spent time in the Salem harbor. When **Joseph Smith** was a boy he spent time with his **Uncle Jesse** in Salem as he recuperated from his leg operation.

Latter-day Saint missionaries came to Salem in the 1830–40s. They included the **Prophet Joseph Smith** and members of the **Quorum of the Twelve.** While here, Joseph received a revelation recorded as D&C 111.

**Lyman R. Sherman** was born in Salem on May 22, 1804, to Asenath Hulbert and Elkanah Sherman. He was ordained one of the first seven Presidents of the Seventy on Feb. 28, 1835 (RPJS 217).

**Amanda Smith,** wife of Warren Smith, was born in Salem on Feb. 22, 1809. She witnessed and left a vivid written account of the Haun's Mill massacre (HiR 83–88).

Elders **Eli P. Maginn** and **Erastus Snow** were prominent and successful missionaries in Salem, organizing a **branch of the Church** here in 1841.

### Historical Sites in Salem

$ ● **1. SALEM WITCH MUSEUM.** At 19½ Washington Square N., on the west corner of **Salem Common,** the museum has life-size dioramas with light and sound depicting the witchcraft hysteria of Salem in 1692. This is a good place to start following the Historic Trail of Salem. South of the Salem Witch Museum is the **Roger Conant statue** (founder of Salem in 1626).

■ **2. UNION STREET.** This street runs for one block from NW to SE between Essex and Derby Streets. It starts near the back of Hawthorne Hotel, which is a short block east of and running parallel with Hawthorne Blvd. This was the location of the **"rented house on Union Street"** where **Joseph Smith, Hyrum Smith, Sidney Rigdon,** and **Oliver Cowdery** lived for their month-long stay in Salem. They left Kirtland on July 25, 1836, stopped in New York City, went by steamer to Providence, RI, then to Boston by steam cars, and finally arrived in Salem on Aug. 4, 1836. They were here to raise money and preach the gospel "door to door" and in public meetings. The city of Salem numbered about 15,000 people at that time.

*Union Street, Salem, MA. Joseph Smith rented a house on this street in 1836. The house in the center of the photo, at 27 Union St., is where author Nathaniel Hawthorne was born. (Photo by Frank Cousin, 1895; courtesy of Essex Institute, Salem, MA.)*

In New York City they consulted creditors concerning their debt and in Salem they were trying to find the "buried treasure" that had been reported in Kirtland by Jonathan Burgess. Burgess met the brethren in Salem, but because of changes he could not tell for certain the house that had the treasure. They found a house they "felt" was the right one on Union Street but failed to find the treasure (ER, Aug. 25, 1836; HC 2:463–64; PWJS 349–50).

A **revelation** (D&C 111) was given to Joseph two days after he and his brethren arrived in Salem. Oliver, Sidney, and Hyrum visited the East India Marine Society Museum that day, leaving Joseph in the solitude of the rented house. It was in this setting that the revelation dated Aug. 6, 1836, was given. The Lord reassured Joseph that although there were "follies" involved with his visit to Salem, there were many "treasures" in this city. Joseph was also promised that he would have power to pay his debts. He was told by the Lord that he should inquire diligently concerning the ancient inhabitants of the city. By 1842 the "treasures," or converts, in Salem numbered 90. The prophecy of the revelation had been fulfilled (HC 2:463–66; SiS 432–37).

**Ezra T. Benson** worked in Salem about a year (Spring 1836–Spring 1837) for the firm of Stoughton and Bilden. He purchased furs and wool, and sold merchandise. He served as an Apostle in the Church (1846–69), and his great-grandson, Ezra Taft Benson, served as an Apostle (1943–85), then as the President of the Church from 1985 to 1994 (BiE 1:99–102; ETB 482–4).

● **3. PICKERING WHARF.** A very attractive waterfront boating, shop-ping, and dining complex is located at the junction of Derby and Union streets. This newly created replica of an old commercial wharf is delightful with its charming atmosphere.

■ **4. THE CUSTOM HOUSE (1819).** The Custom House at 174 Derby Street is part of the Salem Maritime National Historic Site. The historic site also includes the **West India Goods Store,** the **Hawkes House,** the **U.S. Government Bonded Warehouse,** the **Derby House, Derby Wharf, Central Wharf, Hatch's Wharf,** the **Polish Club,** and the **Narbonne-Hale House.**

   Solomon Mack, grandfather of Joseph Smith, served not only in the ground forces of the American army during the Revolu-tionary War, but he also served with his two teenage sons, Solomon and Jason, as sailors on a privateer warship fighting British sloops, schooners, and row-gallies. When Solomon decided to "give up the sea" in 1788 he put in at Salem and "lay sick for weeks." He moved with his family to Gilsum, NH, then, in about 1799, to Tunbridge, VT (JSN 17–18).

   Uncle Jesse Smith's home in Salem provided a haven for the youthful seven- or eight-year-old **Joseph Smith** after his serious leg operation in West Lebanon, NH (ca. 1813). Joseph's parents felt the fresh sea breezes would hasten Joseph's recovery (CHC 1:30). While Joseph was here recovering from his leg operation, Nathaniel Hawthorne was also in Salem with a leg problem. The location of Jesse's home in Salem is unknown.

$ ● **5. DERBY HOUSE (1761).** The oldest brick house in Salem is located just NE of the Custom House on Derby Street. Behind the Derby House on Essex Street is the **Narbonne-Hale House** (1670).

$ ● **6. HOUSE OF THE SEVEN GABLES (1688).** At 54 Turner St. is the birthplace of Salem's favored son **Nathaniel Hawthorne.** This house was made famous by Hawthorne's book *House of the Seven Gables.* North of the House of the Seven Gables at 122 Derby Street is **Ye Olde Pepper Companie,** the "oldest candy company in America." Visitors can watch candy being made.

$ ● **7. CROWNINSHIELD BENTLEY HOUSE (1727).** This house, complete with period furnishings, is located on the corner of Essex Street and Hawthorne Blvd.

$ ● **8. GARDNER-PINGREE HOUSE (1804).** This Federal brick mansion is located at 128 Essex Street next to the Essex Institute.

$ ● **9. ESSEX INSTITUTE.** This complex, including an historical museum, library (inc. genealogy), doll house, shoe shop, stable, and gift shop, is located at 132 Essex Street.

$ ● **10. JOHN WARD HOUSE (1684).** This house, complete with period furnishings, has a weaving room and apothecary. It is located on Brown Street behind the Essex Institute.

● **11. ANDREW SAFFORD HOUSE (1818).** This house is located just east of the John Ward Home at 13 Washington Square West.

$ ■ **12. PEABODY ESSEX MUSEUM.** Located in East India Square on Essex Street (a walking mall street) this museum was founded in 1799 and was known as the East India Marine Society Museum when **Sidney Rigdon, Hyrum Smith,** and **Oliver Cowdery** visited the museum and signed its register on Aug. 5, 1836. Three days later, on Aug. 8, **Joseph Smith** signed the register. The museum features exhibits of the natural history of New England, ethnology, and maritime history.

*Peabody Essex Museum, 136 Essex St., Salem, MA. (1985)*

● **13. SALEM CITY HALL (1837).** On the east side of Washington Street the city hall displays the Indian deed to the town. Eight square miles were purchased for £40 in 1686. **Old Town Hall** and the chamber of commerce is located nearby, just south of the Essex St. Mall at 32 Derby Square.

■ **14. MASONIC HALL, ERASTUS SNOW, AND THE SALEM BRANCH (1841).** The "old" Masonic Hall used by Erastus Snow and the Saints for meetings was located at No. 95 on the NW corner of Essex and

Washington Streets, a block south of the "new" Masonic Hall. On Aug. 10, 1841, Joseph Smith gave directions to members of the Twelve that missionaries be sent to Salem, MA (HC 4:400). **Erastus Snow** and **Benjamin Winchester** were then called to serve here. The Twelve gave Erastus Snow a copy of the "Salem Revelation" (D&C 111) and requested him to fulfill the prophecies made therein. The two elders labored a short time together until Elder Winchester went to Philadelphia. Elder Snow then labored alone. Later his wife joined him and their first son was born here. Elder Erastus Snow began preaching in the "old" Masonic Hall on Sept. 6, 1841. He was so successful, preaching here three or four times during the week and three times on Sundays, that the hall became too small for the crowds.

The small Salem Branch grew to 30 members by Oct. 31, 1841; 53 by Mar. 5, 1842; and 90 by June 1842. The **Salem Branch** was formally organized (again) Mar. 5, 1842, at a conference held in the "old" **Masonic Hall.**

**Elder Eli P. Maginn** had arrived in Nov. 1841, to help Elder Snow in the missionary labors. Maginn debated in the **Mechanic's Hall** for six successive nights against A. C. Comings, anti-Mormon editor of a religious periodical. The debates proved very helpful to Snow's missionary effort. Converts included the debate's moderator, who was an elder in Comings's church. Snow also confronted apostate John C. Bennett, who put in an appearance at Boston and lectured against the Church. Bennett soon found it advisable to leave town. With the exception of a couple of months when he went to Nauvoo, Elder Snow spent over two years laboring in Salem (Sept. 1841–Oct. 1843). Elder Snow served as an Apostle in the Church from 1846 to 1888. He, along with Orson Pratt, became the first Mormons to enter the Salt Lake Valley in 1847 (BiE 1:108–9).

In summarizing Mormon activities in Salem, a local newspaper printed the following: "Mormonism is advancing with a perfect rush in this city, just at present. . . . Meetings have been holden now very frequently for several days past, and crowds flock to listen to the strange doctrines of the 'Latter Day Saints.' . . . We understand that the whole number of those who have come over to the faith, is about eighty" (*The Salem Register,* June 2, 1842).

Apostles **Heber C. Kimball, Lyman Wight,** and **Orson Pratt** held a conference in Salem July 6–8, 1844. The Apostles were in the East preaching the gospel and campaigning for Joseph Smith for president of the United States. At Salem on July 9, Elders Kimball and Wight first heard of the death of the **Prophet Joseph Smith** (HC 7:175).

■ **15. THE LYCEUM.** A hall (now a restaurant) located at 43 Church Street was used by **Joseph Smith, Sidney Rigdon,** and the brethren for **preaching services** in Aug. 1836. The brethren were praised in the press for their good speaking, although they were criticized for their doctrine (SiS 434). The lyceum is also important because the **first long distance phone call** was made from this building by Alexander Graham Bell on Feb. 12, 1877.

■ **16. MECHANIC'S HALL.** Now a YMCA, Mechanic's Hall at 288 Essex Street (NW corner of Essex and Sewell Streets) was the site of a **debate** between **Erastus Snow** and anti-Mormon **A. C. Comings** while the future Apostle Snow labored as a missionary in Salem (BiE 1:108–9).

$ ● **17. PEIRCE-NICHOLS HOUSE (1782).** This historic house is located at 80 Federal Street.

$ ● **18. ASSEMBLY HOUSE (1782).** On Federal Street west of the Peirce-Nichols House, the Assembly House has early furnishings recalling Salem's maritime trade with the Far East.

$ ● **19. ROPES MANSION.** Collections of Nanking porcelain and Irish glass can be seen in this mansion. It is located on Essex Street. Behind the mansion at 316 Essex Street is **First Church**—oldest continuing Protestant society in America and the first to be governed by congregational polity. Roger Williams was pastor of First Church before he fled to Providence, RI, in 1635.

$ ● **20. WITCH HOUSE (1642).** This is the restored home of Jonathan Corwin, a judge of the witchcraft trials in 1692. Here preliminary examinations of persons accused of witchcraft were held. It is located on the NW corner of Essex and North Streets (310½ Essex St.).

$ ● **21. PICKERING HOUSE (1651).** Located at 18 Broad Street is the birthplace of Timothy Pickering, a Salem patriot. This is the **oldest**

**house in Salem,** and has been occupied continuously by the Pickering family.

- **22. CHESTNUT STREET.** This road is one of the most architecturally distinguished streets in America. Many of the mansions that line this street were built by Salem's sea captains in the early 19th century. The mansion facing the twin elms is the **Phillips House.**

- **23. SALEM MARKETPLACE.** On New Derby Street, this marketplace has individual brick stalls for merchandising.

$ ● **24. PIONEER VILLAGE.** This is a reproduction of buildings typical of Salem in the 1630s. It has pioneer industries, a pillory, stocks, etc. It is located at Forest River Park on the oceanfront in the southern part of the city. Travel south on Lafayette Street to West Ave., then east a short distance.

■ **BEVERLY**

Just north of Salem on State 1A across the Danvers River is Beverly, where **Orson Hyde** and **Samuel Smith** preached the gospel in 1832. Orson noted that "a numerous crowd came out and fired crackers during the meeting and made disturbance, and after the meeting the rabble set up a hue and cry through the town and round the house like a pack of grizzly wolves determined to devour us" (OrH 26). The crowd finally dispersed when the owner of the house in which the meeting was held "told them that if they did not go away that he had powder and shot and would clear the yard" (OrH 31).

■ **TOPSFIELD—Smith Ancestral Home for Five Generations**

Topsfield village is located just off U.S. 1 on State 97 about 20 miles north of Boston, near the center of Topsfield Township. It is 1½ miles east of I-95.

The earliest settlers in the area came from England and moved into Topsfield in 1641. In the colonial period most of Topsfield's residents earned a living by farming. Some of the farmers became involved in the witchcraft episode of the 1690s. In 1990 Topsfield had approximately 5,000 residents and served as a bedroom city for Boston.

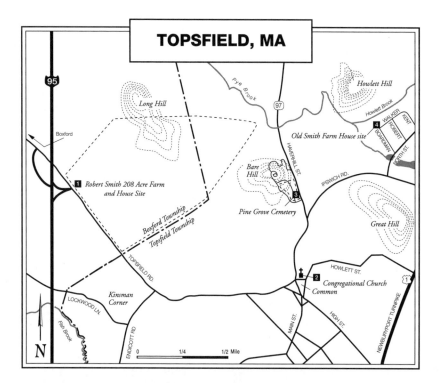

TOPSFIELD, MA

Topsfield is of interest to Latter-day Saints because it is the ancestral home of the **Prophet Joseph Smith.** Five generations of Joseph Smith's paternal ancestors lived and farmed in Topsfield and Boxford Townships: Robert Smith, Samuel Smith I, Samuel Smith II, Asael Smith, and Joseph Smith Sr.

**Brigham Young** also had ancestors in Topsfield. Through his mother, Abigail Howe, Brigham was related to Francis Peabody, who built the gristmill on Pye Brook and lived a quarter of a mile from the old Smith farmhouse. Francis Peabody was also an ancestor of the Prophet Joseph Smith, who was a sixth cousin to Brigham Young.

Places of interest in Topsfield include the following:

■ **1. THE OLD SMITH HOMESTEAD. Robert Smith** came from Boston, England to Boston, MA, in 1638. He was about 14 years old. In 1648 he moved to Ipswich where he met and married a local girl, Mary French.

In 1661 Robert and Mary moved to Boxford Township where they purchased a 208-acre farm "lying partly in Topsfield [Township] and partly in Boxford [Township]" (1.3 miles WNW of the

Topsfield Common and halfway between Boxford and Topsfield Villages). This farm became known as the "Smith Homestead." Since Robert's family attended church in Topsfield, they were known as the "Smiths of Topsfield." Robert and Mary had ten children; the last eight were born in Boxford Township (HiB 33–35; DOB 49–50; Wills, deeds, etc. at Brigham Young University Library). (Consult the map for the approximate location of the farm and house.)

After Robert's death in 1693, his son **Samuel** I moved from Boxford Township to Topsfield Village where, after marrying Rebecca Curtis in 1707, he raised his family.

■  **2. THE CONGREGATIONAL CHURCH OF TOPSFIELD.** The church is located opposite the common on State 97 in the center of the village. This is the site where Joseph Smith's ancestors were baptized and where they worshipped. **Asael** was baptized here on Mar. 11, 1744, and **Joseph Smith Sr.** was also baptized here. Residents of Topsfield built the first meetinghouse in 1663, a second one in the 1700s, and the present one in 1846—all on the same site.

■  **3. PINE GROVE CEMETERY.** Located on the west side of State 97 and ½ mile north of Topsfield Common is the cemetery. It contains the graves of **Robert Smith, Samuel Smith I,** and **Samuel Smith II.** The exact location of these graves is unknown, but a Smith family marker in remembrance of the Smiths buried here was erected in 1873 under the direction of George A. Smith, counselor to Brigham Young. The obelisk marker is about six feet high. It is located about 145' north of the SE corner and about 28' west of the rock wall.

*Smith Family Marker,*
*Topsfield, MA. (1975)*

■  **4. OLD SMITH FARMHOUSE SITE.** This is the birthplace of Asael and Joseph Smith Sr. The old Smith farmhouse site is located on Pye, or Peabody, Brook 1¼ miles NE of the Topsfield Common on the corner of Boardman and Walker Streets. On the very same site a beautiful white 19th century (1876) New England-style home has been built. The home is owned by Levi C. Wade Jr. An original well exists in back of the home.

Five generations of Smiths lived on the old Smith homestead, and four generations lived in the old Smith farmhouse: Samuel I, Samuel II, Asael, and Joseph Smith Sr.

*Old Smith Farmhouse Site, Topsfield, MA. (1973)*

Asael, the Prophet Joseph Smith's grandfather, made the "big move" in 1791 when he left the old Smith homestead and moved first to Ipswich for six months, and then to **Tunbridge,** VT, where Joseph Smith Sr. met his future bride, Lucy Mack.

*Old Smith Farmhouse, Topsfield, MA.*
*Four generations of Smiths lived in this house, including Joseph Smith Sr. Built in 1860.*
*(Before 1875)*

In 1870 a missionary, Elder N. H. Felt, visited Topsfield and described the old Smith home, which was still standing. He noted the "old beaded oak beams and the high unique fireplace, five or six feet high, by four feet wide, O.G. jams and bricks, herring-boned for ornament on the back; all showing for that day, a good deal of taste" (DN Feb. 2, 1870). The house was torn down between 1870 and 1875 (JSN 89–100; BOM 20–22; BYUS Autumn 1973, pp. 56–76).

## ■ BOXFORD (ROWLEY)—Birthplace of Mary Duty

Located three miles NW of Topsfield and about 1½ miles NW of the 208-acre old Smith homestead, purchased by Robert and Mary Smith in 1661, is the small village of Boxford, formerly known as Rowley.

Joseph Smith's grandmother **Mary Duty,** wife of Asael Smith, was born here Oct. 11, 1743 (JSN 191; ENS Feb. 1971, p. 18).

■ **IPSWICH—Home of Robert Smith, Mary French, Asael Smith, and Richard Kimball**

Twenty-five miles NE of Boston on State 1A is the small city of Ipswich, where three important men of Mormon history lived. It was settled by John Winthrop Jr. in 1633, and the Pilgrim fathers had even thought of settling here.

**Robert Smith,** great-great-great-grandfather of the Prophet Joseph Smith, moved from Boston to Ipswich and lived here for 13 years. From Ipswich, Robert and his wife, Mary, moved to Rowley Township (now Boxford) near Topsfield in 1661 and purchased a 208-acre farm that became known as the "Smith Homestead" (LJFS 16–17).

**Asael Smith,** great-grandson of Robert and grandfather of Joseph Smith, settled his father's estate in Topsfield and then moved to Ipswich in the early spring of 1791, where he leased both land for farming and a dairy herd for milking. Asael's stay of about six months was terminated when he learned of inexpensive land in Tunbridge, VT, where he moved in Oct. 1791 (JSN 100–1; BOM 22).

**Richard Kimball,** great-great-great-great-grandfather of Heber C. Kimball, moved with his wife, Ursula Scott, to Ipswich from Watertown (Cambridge) in 1637. His "house lot" adjoined "Goodwin Simmons at the west end of the town." Kimball evidently died here on Mar. 1, 1676 (LHCK 506–7).

■ **GEORGETOWN (NEW ROWLEY)—Birthplace of Henry Harriman**

Located 6 miles north and a little west of Topsfield on State 97 is Georgetown (New Rowley).

In 1832 there was a **branch of the Church** in New Rowley. **Henry Harriman,** one of the first seven Presidents of Seventy (1838–91), was born here June 9, 1804 (BiE 1:193).

■ **BRADFORD—Home of Heber C. Kimball's Ancestors**

Bradford is located on the south side of the Merrimack River on State 125 immediately south of Haverhill. **Heber C. Kimball's** paternal ances-

*John F. Boynton*

try of four generations were born and raised here (ABM 135–40).

**John F. Boynton,** one of the original Twelve Apostles (1835–37), was born here on Sep. 20, 1811. He was baptized in 1832 by Joseph Smith, excommunicated in 1837, visited Brigham Young in Salt Lake City in 1872, and died out of the Church in Syracuse, NY, in 1890 (BiE 1:91; HiR 53).

**Leonard W. Hardy,** first counselor to Bishop Edward Hunter (1856–83) and to Wm. B. Preston (1884), was born here on Dec. 31, 1805 (BiE 1:236).

A **conference** was held in the Bradford Branch on Aug. 7, 1835, with nine of the Twelve present (HC 2:241–42).

■ SALISBURY—**Home of John Mack and Benjamin Kimball**

The most northeastern village in Massachusetts is Salisbury, located 15 miles NE of Topsfield on U.S. 1.

**John Mack,** great-great-grandfather of the Prophet Joseph Smith, sailed from Scotland and landed at Boston Harbor in 1680. He was about age 18. He moved to Salisbury where he lived with his wife, **Sarah Bagley.** Sarah's father, Orlando, a constable in Amesbury, arrested Susannah Martin because she "bewitched" some cows. Susannah was tried and executed. The incident was later celebrated in one of Whittier's poems (LAP 24). After John and Sarah had their first child they moved to Concord, MA, and then to Lyme, CT, where they gave birth to their twelfth child. Lyme became the "Mack Homestead."

# South and Southeast of Boston

● QUINCY—**Adams National Historic Site**

Located on the bay in the SE corner of greater Boston, on State 3A, is Quincy, the birthplace of U.S. Presidents John and John Quincy Adams. They were born in cottages on the same block.

■ PLYMOUTH

Plymouth, one of the earliest permanent colonial settlements in

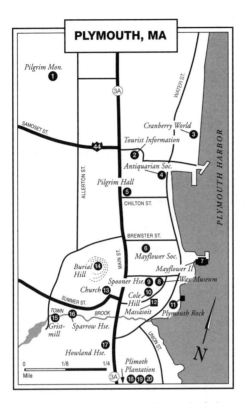

the U.S., is located on Cape Cod Bay 40 miles SE of Boston on State 3A. It was founded in Dec. 1620 by survivors of the Mayflower. Indians of the Wampanoag and Algonquian tribes helped the struggling colony survive by teaching the Pilgrims how to farm corn and new fishing techniques. By 1720 there was a population of 2,000 in Plymouth, and by 1830 a population of 5,000. There were 100 sailing vessels in the harbor by the latter date. The Plymouth Cordage Company was the largest rope manufacturer in the world. Today Plymouth is mainly a tourist town with many historical sites.

Apostate **John C. Bennett** moved to the vicinity of Plymouth after following James Jesse Strang for several years. Here he practiced dentistry, medicine, and poultry farming. He later moved to Polk Co., IA, where he died Aug. 5, 1867. He had been the mayor of Nauvoo, the university chancellor, and an assistant to Joseph Smith before being excommunicated in 1842.

Walking is the best way to see Plymouth, but there is also the Plymouth Trolley that visits important sites as far away as Plimoth Plantation.

### *Historical Sites in Plymouth*

Listed from North to South

- **1. FOREFATHERS MONUMENT.** This monument, located on Allerton Street, one block west of State 3A on the north end of the city, stands 81 feet tall.
- **2. TOURIST INFORMATION BOOTHS.** Located at the intersection of

State 44 (Samoset St.) and Court Street (State 3A) near *Mayflower II*, are information booths.

- **3. CRANBERRY WORLD VISITOR'S CENTER.** This site on Water Street north of the **town wharf** depicts the history of cranberries through a diorama, A-V programs, cooking demonstrations, and outdoor working cranberry bogs.

$ ● **4. HEDGE HOUSE (1809).** The building at 126 Water Street was a shipowner's house.

$ ● **5. PILGRIM HALL MUSEUM (1824).** The nation's oldest historical museum, at 27 Court Street, houses actual possessions of the Pilgrim Fathers. It is a superb research library.

$ ● **6. MAYFLOWER SOCIETY HOUSE (1754).** The house at 4 Winslow Street was built by Edward Winslow, great-grandson of the Pilgrim governor, John Carver.

$ ■ **7. *MAYFLOWER II*.** A full-scale reproduction of the original *Mayflower* is at Frazier State Pier, Water Street. It was built in England and sailed across the Atlantic in 1957. Visitors can feel the size of the boat and sense the feelings the little band of 102 passengers and 25 crewmen must have had as they spent 66 days on the sea before finally arriving in America on Dec. 21, 1620.

Seven ancestors of the **Prophet Joseph Smith** were on the *Mayflower,* including John Howland, Edward Fuller, and John Tillery. These three signed the Mayflower Compact. **John Howland,** fifth great-grandfather of Joseph Smith and 13th signer, was for a time a servant to John Carver, the first governor of Plymouth Colony. Four of the seven, Edward Fuller, John Tillery, and their wives were counted with the 44 who died that first winter—44 out of 102 Pilgrims! Near *Mayflower II* on Water Street are the **First House** and **1627 House,** typical structures of the 1620–27 period.

$ ● **8. PLYMOUTH NATIONAL WAX MUSEUM.** The museum on Cole's Hill has 150 wax figures in 26 lifelike scenes that tell the Pilgrim story.

$ ● **9. SPOONER HOUSE (1749).** The Spooner House at 27 North Street near Cole's Hill is filled with antiques. It was lived in by the same family for over 200 years.

● **10. COLE'S HILL.** West of Plymouth Rock is the site of a secret burial ground where corn was planted over the graves so that the Indians could not easily determine how many settlers had died during the first year of settlement. Rainstorms exposed the bones, which were then placed in a **sarcophagus.** Just south of Cole's Hill is **Brewster Gardens** with the **town brook.** It was in this brook that herring were caught for fertilizing the corn. The reeds that grow on the banks were used for roof thatching.

● **11. PLYMOUTH ROCK.** "Cornerstone of the Nation," Plymouth Rock is located on Water Street under a canopy on the shore where the Pilgrims arrived Dec. 21, 1620.

■ **12. MASSASOIT STATUE.** *Massasoit,* by sculptor Cyrus E. Dallin of Springville, UT, is located SW of Plymouth Rock on Cole's Hill. Duplicates of this statue stand in front of the Utah State Capitol and near the Brigham Young University library. Massasoit was a chief of the Wampanoag tribe of Indians. He made a peace treaty with Governor John Carver of Plymouth Colony in the spring of 1621. Massasoit and a number of his braves joined the Pilgrims for their first Thanksgiving Day in the fall of 1621.

● **13. FIRST PARISH CHURCH.** The site of the Pilgrims' church is located on Leyden Street. The original was built in 1683, and the present church, built in 1897, is the fifth on the site.

● **14. BURIAL HILL.** This cemetery is located up the stone steps north of the First Parish Church. It overlooks the square. The first fort was built here in 1621 and contained five cannons. The small red brick structure was the powder magazine. The fort was used as a meeting house and burial ground. The graves of Governor Bradford, Edward Grey, Thomas Clark, and John Cotton are located here.

$ ● **15. JENNEY GRISTMILL.** Located on the town brook at Spring Lane is a replica of an early American water-powered gristmill. It is in daily operation grinding corn into meal as the Pilgrims did. Demonstrations of pioneer craft work are also available.

$ ● **16. RICHARD SPARROW HOUSE (1640).** Located at 42 Summer St., this is the oldest house in Plymouth, and is one of the oldest wooden dwellings in the United States. Potters demonstrate their craft as they work here. Near this site is the renovated **1749 Court House.**

$ ● **17. JABEZ HOWLAND HOUSE (1666).** Located on Sandwich St., this is the only house now standing in Plymouth where Pilgrims are known to have lived. Active crafts are featured.

$ ● **18. HARLOW OLD FORT HOUSE (1677).** The house at 119 Sandwich St. is built of timber taken from the first Pilgrim fort. Staff reenactors spin flax and wool, weave using historic looms, make bayberry candles, and demonstrate early domestic arts.

● **19. HARLOW-HOLMES HOMESTEAD.**

$ ● **20. PLIMOTH PLANTATION.** This living outdoor history museum is located 2 ½ miles south of Plymouth Rock on State 3A. It is a replica of the Pilgrim settlement of 1627. In this full-scale village costumed guides play the parts of the Pilgrims, show their crafts and trades, and discuss concerns of the 1620s using old English mannerisms.

■ **CAPE COD**

Cape Cod is a narrow neck of land that extends east then north and creates a large bay about 25 miles wide and 25 miles long. Cape Cod is separated from mainland Massachusetts by Cape Cod Canal, and the tip of the cape is about 75 miles by land from Plymouth.

Although fishing, lobstering, boat building, and cranberry raising are very important economically to the Cape, tourism is by far the largest industry. Beaches, New England architecture, pine trees, rolling dunes, and a mild ocean climate make the cape one of the most popular vacation spots in America. A few interesting places to visit include:

**1. SANDWICH.** Sandwich is the oldest town on Cape Cod. It is very charming.

**2. HYANNIS.** This town serves as the commercial hub for tourism on Cape Cod.

**3. HYANNIS PORT.** Located at Hyannis Port is the Kennedy family compound.

**4. DENNIS.** From Scargo Hill in Dennis you can have a spectacular view of Cape Cod Bay.

**5. CHATHAM.** Chatham is a typical, commercial-free Cape Cod village. At about noon, fishing boats unload their catches at Fish Pier.

**6. PROVINCETOWN.** This settlement has a quarrel with Plymouth because the Pilgrims actually landed here first, staying at Provincetown four or five weeks before going to Plymouth.

In Mar. 1844 **Wilford Woodruff** organized a branch of the Church at Cape Cod with 21 members. He returned to Cape Cod in the fall of 1849 where he preached and also healed an 84-year-old lady (WW 338–39).

■ **MARTHA'S VINEYARD**

From Woods Hole at the SW tip of Cape Cod, or from Hyannis Port, one can catch a ferry and go across Nantucket Sound to the island of Martha's Vineyard. The main port of Martha's Vineyard is at Vineyard Haven. The island is a summer resort like its neighbor island, Nantucket, 20 miles to the east.

**William Weeks,** architect of the Nauvoo Temple in Nauvoo, IL, was born on Martha's Vineyard, Apr. 11, 1813. Weeks drew the plans to the Nauvoo Temple and designed its baptismal font, personally carving the first of the twelve oxen that supported it. The remaining oxen were carved by Elijah Fordham (DHS 1:162; BYUS Spring 1979, pp. 337–59).

■ **FAIRHAVEN—Birthplace of John C. Bennett**

About 50 miles south of Boston along U.S. 6 and on the shores of the Atlantic Ocean (Apponagansett Bay) is Fairhaven, birthplace of **John C. Bennett.**

Born Aug. 4, 1804, Bennett joined the Mormons in Nauvoo in 1840. He was well educated and was the first dean of the medical school of Willoughby University near Kirtland. He attained popularity and power in Nauvoo second only to that of Joseph Smith. He was mayor of Nauvoo, "acting counselor" in the First Presidency, chancellor of the University of Nauvoo, major general of the Nauvoo Legion, and president of the Nauvoo Agricultural and

Manufacturing Association. Bennett was excommunicated from the Church in 1842. He wrote a bitter anti-Mormon book and settled in Plymouth for a time where he practiced medicine and became a breeder of poultry. Bennett died Aug. 5, 1868, in Iowa and is buried in Polk City (NAU 113–14; D&C 124:16–17; ABM 10–14).

■ NEW BEDFORD

Located about 50 miles south of Boston along U.S. 6 and on the shores of the Atlantic Ocean (Apponagansett Bay) is New Bedford. From the city's harbor on Oct. 9, 1843, Elders **Noah Rogers, Addison Pratt, B. F. Grouard,** and **K. Hanks** set sail on their first mission to the Society Islands of the South Pacific. They paid $100 each for passage on the ship *Timoleon* (T&S 6:1085). **Wilford Woodruff** was laboring here as a missionary when on Oct. 26, 1848, he read of the burning of the Nauvoo Temple (WW 334).

New Bedford has a **whaling museum.**

## West and Southwest of Boston

■ DEDHAM—**Fairbanks Homestead**

Located 10 miles SW of the Boston city center on U.S. 1 is Dedham, the homestead of Puritan settler Johnathan Fairbanks, an ancestor—ten generations back—of Avard Fairbanks, famous Salt Lake City sculptor. The homestead was built in 1636 and is said to be the oldest standing homestead in America.

■ MARLBOROUGH—**Home of Brigham Young's Ancestors**

Located 25 miles west of Boston on U.S. 20 is Marlborough, home of the Brigham family, ancestors of Brigham Young. Samuel Brigham, born in 1689, was one of a group of 40 persons who purchased Grafton, MA, from the Indians.

■ HOLLISTON—**Birthplace of Albert P. Rockwood, Elizabeth Haven Barlow, and Maria S. Haven**

Located 24 miles SW of Boston on State 16 is the small town of

*Albert Perry Rockwood*

Holliston, birthplace of **Albert P. Rockwood,** one of the first seven Presidents of the First Quorum of Seventy from 1845 to 1879. He was born June 5, 1805 (BiE 194). In 1811 **Willard Richards** moved here with his parents as a six-year-old. They lived here one year then moved to Richmond (InD 21). **Brigham Young** and **Willard Richards** organized a branch of the Church here in March–May 1837. **Parley P. Pratt** taught in the townhouse here in the fall of 1837 and baptized two people. The branch numbered 16 members in Aug. 1839 (HC 4:6).

**Elizabeth Haven Barlow** was born and raised in Holliston. Elizabeth married **Israel Barlow** at Quincy, IL, and later settled with her husband in West Bountiful, UT (WV 106–15; BiE 4:687).

**Ellen Rockwood,** who became a plural wife of Brigham Young, was born here in 1829.

**Maria S. Haven** was born in Holliston to John Haven and Judith Temple. Maria married **Robert T. Burton,** a colonel of the Mormon militia in the Utah War of 1857–58.

■ HOPKINTON—**Home of the parents of Brigham Young, Heber C. Kimball, Willard Richards, and many other early Mormons. Starting point of the Boston Marathon.**

Twenty-five miles SW of Boston on State 135 is Hopkinton, home of the parents of Brigham Young, Heber C. Kimball, and Willard Richards. These three men became the First Presidency of the Church in 1847. **William Young,** Brigham Young's great-grandfather moved to Hopkinton about 1740. He bought two pieces of land—115- and 100-acre parcels. He built his home on the 115-acre piece that included the junction of Elm and Lumber Streets and extended easterly and southerly as far as Chamberlain Street. The 100-acre parcel extended from the present Elm Street SE along South Street.

**Dr. Joseph Young,** grandfather of Brigham Young, settled here after serving as a surgeon in the French and Indian War. Here he met and married Elizabeth Hayden Treadway (HIB 13–14).

**John Young,** father of Brigham Young, was born here Mar. 7, 1763. He married Abigail (Nabby) Howe on Oct. 31, 1785, at Hopkinton. Their first eight children were born in Hopkinton. Their

*Joseph Young*

homesite was on Saddle Hill near Basin Lake or reservoir no. 4 of the Boston Metropolitan Water District (InD 587). In Jan. 1801, John and Abigail moved to Whitingham, VT, where child number nine, **Brigham Young,** was born on June 1, 1801. Brigham's older brothers and sisters, **Nancy, Fanny, Rhoda, John Jr., Nabby, Susannah, Joseph,** and **Phineas Howe** were all born in Hopkinton.

**Peter Howe** and his wife, **Thankful,** were the great-grandparents of Brigham Young, Willard Richards, and Albert Perry Rockwood, who was one of the first Presidents of Seventy (1845–79). Peter's son **Phineas Howe** was Brigham Young's grandfather. Phineas married **Susannah Goddard.** They lived in Hopkinton on Howe Street beside the bridge over Indian Brook. They had ten children all born in Hopkinton. Of the ten, three daughters became Mormons and married men who became leaders in the Church: (1) **Rhoda** married **Joseph Richards** and they were parents of **Willard** and **Phineas Richards;** (2) **Abigail** (Nabby) married **John Young,** father of Brigham Young—all of their children, except one who died in infancy, became Mormons; (3) **Betty** married **John Haven** and they had eight children—their first, Betsy, married **Israel Barlow,** their seventh, Nancy, married **Albert Perry Rockwood.**

**Solomon F. Kimball,** father of Heber C. Kimball, was born here in 1770 (HCKM 4).

**Willard Richards,** second counselor to Brigham Young from 1847 to 1854, was born in Hopkinton on June 24, 1804, to Joseph and Rhoda Richards—their eleventh and last child.

■ MENDON—**Birthplace of Ezra T. Benson, Apostle 1846–69**

*Ezra T. Benson
(Courtesy LDSCA)*

Mendon is a small town 32 miles SW of Boston on State 16. Here **Ezra T. Benson** was born to John and Chloe Benson on Feb. 22, 1811. His great-grandson, Ezra Taft Benson, became President of the Church on Nov. 11, 1985 (BiE 1:100; HiR 132; ETB 482–84).

■ **UXBRIDGE—Home of Ezra T. Benson, Apostle 1846–69**

Uxbridge is located five miles SW of Mendon on State 16. At age sixteen (1827), **Ezra T. Benson** came here to live with his sister and her husband who were keeping a hotel in the center of town. He lived here three years (BiE 1:100).

■ **NORTHBRIDGE—Home of Pamelia Andrus, wife of Ezra T. Benson, Apostle 1846–69**

Located 12 miles SE of Worcester on State 122 is Northbridge, where Ezra T. Benson's wife Pamelia Andrus lived. They were married in 1832 (MHBY 245; ETB 2; BiE 1:100).

The first branch of the Church in Northbridge was organized in 1840 by Elder Joseph Ball (T&S 2:253).

■ **OAKHAM—Birthplace of Joseph Knight Sr.**

Fourteen miles NW of Worcester and two miles SW of State 122 is Oakham, where **Joseph Knight Sr.,** was born Nov. 3, 1772. In 1809, he moved to Bainbridge then Colesville in New York. Joseph Smith, the prophet, was employed by Joseph Knight Sr., in Colesville about 1824. Later, as Joseph translated the Book of Mormon in Harmony, PA, Joseph Knight Sr., brought provisions to him. A special revelation, **Section 12 of the Doctrine and Covenants,** was directed to Joseph Knight Sr., in 1829. Later he became one of the first persons baptized into the Church (BiE 2:772–73; BYUS Autumn 1976, p. 29).

■ **PETERSHAM—Birthplace of Emmeline B. Wells**

*Emmeline B. Wells, ca 1879.*
*(Courtesy LDSCA)*

About 14 miles NW of Oakham on State 122 is Petersham, where **Emmeline B. Wells** was born Feb. 29, 1828, to David and Deiadama Woodward. Emmeline graduated from a girls' school at age 15 and then became a teacher. She joined the Church and later married Newel K. Whitney as a plural wife. After Newell's death she married Daniel H. Wells. She was the editor of *Woman's Exponent* from 1877 to 1914, and general president of the Relief Society from 1910 to 1921 (WV 292–306; ABM 382–85).

$ ● STURBRIDGE—**"Old Sturbridge Village"**

Fifty-eight miles SW of Boston and 18 miles SW of Worcester on U.S. 20 (two miles south of MA Turnpike–U.S. 90) is Sturbridge, where an outdoor living history museum, **Old Sturbridge Village,** is located. It consists of 36 old original houses surrounding a green on a 200-acre site. Costumed guides explain typical village life and crafts in a rural New England town during the 1830s.

■ HOLLAND—**Home of Ezra T. Benson, Apostle 1846–69**

Holland is located about three miles north of the Connecticut state line and seven miles SW of Sturbridge. **Ezra T. Benson** moved here from Uxbridge about 1834. Here he and his wife's brother hired a cotton factory from Elbridge G. Fuller. The cotton business was not successful so he "took" a hotel here. He served as postmaster until the spring of 1837 when he moved to Salem. After a short time there he went west. By 1840 he had settled in Quincy, IL, where he heard the gospel and was baptized a Mormon (BiE 1:100; ETB 2).

■ SPRINGFIELD—**Birthplace of Levi W. Hancock, Seventy 1835–82**

Located on the Connecticut River in SW Massachusetts where I-90 and I-91 cross is Springfield, the city where **Levi W. Hancock** was born Apr. 7, 1803, to Thomas Hancock and Amy Ward. He was baptized by Parley P. Pratt in 1830 (HC 1:322) and was chosen as one of the first seven Presidents of the First Quorum of Seventy in 1838. He held this office for 47 years until his death in 1882 in Washington, UT. Levi was a bodyguard for

*Levi W. Hancock*

Joseph Smith and was the only General Authority that enlisted in the Mormon Battalion. He was a pioneer settler of Manti, UT (BiE 1:188).

**Israel Barlow** was born Sept. 13, 1806, to Jonathan Barlow and Annis Gillet in **Granville,** 17 miles west of Springfield on State 57.

■ BELCHERTOWN (BELCHER)—**Birthplace of Orrin Porter Rockwell**

*Orrin Porter Rockwell*

Eighteen miles NE of Springfield on U.S. 202 is the town where **Orrin Porter Rockwell** was born on June 28, 1813. His parents were Orrin Rockwell and Sarah Witt. When Porter was four years old, his family moved to Manchester, NY. Porter's distant relative Joseph Smith lived just a mile from the Rockwells. Porter became a very good friend of Joseph Smith and worked at odd jobs—picking berries and cutting firewood—after his own chores at home, to raise money to help pay for the printing of the Book of Mormon. Porter was one of the very first converts baptized into the newly organized Church of Jesus Christ of Latter-day Saints. He died in Salt Lake City, June 9, 1878. He was baptized at age 16 and was at that time the youngest member of the Church (HC 1:79). When he died he was the oldest member of the Church in terms of fellowship (OPR 3–5, 366; ABM 249–53).

■ HADLEY, SOUTH HADLEY, AND SUNDERLAND—**Lovisa Mack Tuttle's Home**

Hadley and South Hadley are located respectively 20 and 10 miles north of Springfield on State 116 and 47. It was in this area that **Lovisa Mack,** Joseph Smith's aunt, lived with her husband, Joseph Tuttle, after their marriage on Jan. 31, 1780. Here a sick Lovisa was nursed for two years by her sister **Lovina.** Lovisa was miraculously healed "of the Lord" in nearby **Sunderland** (nine miles north of Hadley on State 47) in 1791. Later in the week of her healing she bore testimony of the miracle to an audience of the village church in Sunderland. After this experience Lovisa lived in Hadley until her death in 1794.

Near the time that Lovisa had her miraculous healing, Lovina became very ill. During her illness her sister **Lucy** cared for her day and night. In 1794 Solomon Mack traveled from Gilsum to take his daughter Lovina "home" where she could get parental care. The two had traveled only 4 miles to the area of **Montague** when Lovina died at Taft's Inn. Solomon took her body to Gilsum, where Lovina was buried beside her sister Lovisa—both having died that same year of 1794 (HJS 12–20; JSN 18–19, 63–87).

■ **MONTAGUE—Home of Solomon Mack and Birthplace of Isaac Morley**

Montague is a small town located near the Connecticut River west of State 63, 15 miles south of the Vermont border and 30 miles north of Springfield. This was the home of **Solomon Mack's family** for about 14 years from 1778 to 1792. Solomon was the Prophet Joseph Smith's grandfather.

**Elisha Mack,** Solomon's brother, also lived here. He ran a sawmill in Greenfield and built a dam at Turner's Falls, five miles to the north (HJS 12–20, JSN 18–19, 63–87).

*Isaac Morley*

**Isaac Morley** was born a son of Thos. E. Morley and Edith Marsh in Montague on Mar. 11, 1786.

He became the first "first counselor" to the first bishop of the Church in Kirtland, OH, and served in that position from 1831 to 1840. He was ordained patriarch of Far West in 1837 by Joseph Smith, Sidney Rigdon, and Hyrum Smith. Isaac came west with the pioneers, settled in Sanpete County, UT, and died in Fairview, UT, in 1865 (BiE 1:235–36).

● **DEERFIELD—Historic Deerfield**

Located three miles south of Greenfield on U.S. 5 is a restored village of houses dating to the 1600s.

■ **GREENFIELD—Birthplace of Titus Billings**

Located 12 miles south of the New Hampshire border on I-91 is Greenfield, where **Titus Billings** was born Mar. 25, 1793. He was the second person baptized in Kirtland, OH, in Nov. 1830 (HC 1:266). Billings was appointed the second "second counselor" to Bishop Edward Partridge, first bishop of the Church. He served in this capacity from 1837 to 1840. John Corrill had been the first "second counselor" from 1831 to 1837 (BiE 1:242).

■ BECKET—**Birthplace of Eliza R. Snow**

Located 12 miles SE of Pittsfield, Berkshire Co., on State 8 is Becket, birthplace of "Zion's Poetess," **Eliza Roxey Snow.** She was secretary of the first Relief Society and later general president of the same women's organization. She was born Jan. 21, 1804, eleven months before the Prophet Joseph Smith to whom she was later sealed in marriage. In the Church she is particularly famous for having written the words to the hymn "O My Father!"

*Eliza R. Snow*
*(Courtesy LDSCA)*

After Joseph Smith's death, Eliza married Brigham Young in 1849. Her brother, Lorenzo, became President and prophet of The Church of Jesus Christ of Latter-day Saints in 1898 (BiE 1:693–97; ABM 320–25).

● **STOCKBRIDGE**

Chesterwood, the studio of **Daniel Chester French,** sculptor of the Minute Man statue of Concord and the Lincoln Memorial statue at Washington DC, is located at Stockbridge, five miles SE of West Stockbridge on State 102.

■ WEST STOCKBRIDGE—**Birthplace of Daniel and Orson Spencer**

Located in the extreme west end of Massachusetts, 2 ½ miles east of the New York border on I-90, is the town of West Stockbridge, where two stalwart defenders of The Church of Jesus Christ of Latter-day Saints were born: **Daniel and Orson Spencer.** Ten miles to the NW is **Canaan,** NY, home of **Orson Pratt, Parley P. Pratt,** and **John Van Cott.**

**Daniel Spencer** was born July 20, 1794, in West Stockbridge to Daniel Spencer and Chloe Wilson. When Daniel heard of Mormonism, he closed his business for two weeks and studied the new faith. One day, when his son was with him in his study, he suddenly burst into tears and exclaimed: "My God, the

*Daniel Spencer*

thing is true, and as an honest man I must

embrace it; but it will cost me all I have got on earth" (BiE 1:287). Daniel was baptized, and it was only a short time until a branch of the Church was organized with Daniel presiding. He emigrated to Utah as a "captain of fifty" in 1847, and later served as the president of the Salt Lake Stake (1849–53, 1856–68).

*Orson Spencer*

**Orson Spencer** was born in West Stockbridge on Mar. 14, 1802. He attended the academy in nearby Lenox and graduated from Union College at Schenectady, NY, with high honors in 1824. He then taught at an academy in Georgia and studied law. In 1827 he joined the Baptist Church, then studied at and graduated from Hamilton Literary and Technological College in 1829. He served as an "extensively known" Baptist preacher for twelve years until his brother Daniel baptized him into the LDS Church in the spring of 1841. He cast his lot with the Saints in Nauvoo and headed west over the plains in 1846. Because of their poor circumstances, Orson's wife, Catherine, had asked her parents to support them with financial aid. They had refused because of Catherine's newly-found faith. As she and her husband crossed the state of Iowa with the pioneers, a heavenly messenger appeared to her and told her she had suffered enough. She died near Keosauqua, IA, and was carried back to Nauvoo for burial. Orson was left with six children to rear—all under 14 years of age. One of those children, Aurelia (Rogers), became the first president of the Church's Primary Association in 1878.

Orson Spencer presided over the British Mission (1847–49), edited the *Millennial Star,* and wrote a series of letters to the Reverend Crowel, which were published in 1848 as *Spencer's Letters.* In 1850 he was appointed the first chancellor of the University of Deseret (University of Utah) where he served until his death in 1855 (BiE 337–39; MoP 73–75; CHC 4:117).

■ **RICHMOND—Willard Richard's Home and Franklin D. Richard's Birthplace**

Located two miles from the New York border and three miles north of West Stockbridge on State 41 is Richmond, home of Willard and Franklin D. Richards.

**Willard Richards** was born June 24, 1804, at Hopkinton, MA,

*Willard Richards*
*(Courtesy RLDSLA)*

and at age ten moved with his parents, Joseph and Rhoda, to Richmond near the western border of Massachusetts. The Joseph Richards home was still standing and owned by Ernest Thomas in the 1940s. It was located on the west side of Dublin Road where Mill Creek flows under the road near the southern boundary of Richmond. The **pool** below the bridge is the place where **Franklin D. Richards** was baptized by his father, **Phineas.** The house had some additions but in the 1950s it was much the same as it was when Joseph Richards built it and lived there with his family (InD 116–17).

Willard investigated "religion" and was convinced that the "sects were all wrong." In 1835 he obtained a Book of Mormon at his cousin Lucius Parker's house in Southborough. Before reading half a page he declared, "God or the devil has had a hand in that book, for man never wrote it" (InD 601). In 1836 he was baptized by Brigham Young at Kirtland. In 1837 he went on a mission to England. While on his mission in 1838 he met and married Jennetta Richards. He was ordained an Apostle in 1840. As a private secretary to Joseph Smith, he was with the prophet in **Carthage Jail** at the martyrdom. Willard served as second counselor to Brigham Young from 1847 to his death in 1854. He served as editor and proprietor of the *Deseret News,* as Church Historian, and as postmaster of Salt Lake City (BiE 1:34–37).

*Franklin D. Richards*
*(1852)*

**Franklin D. Richards** was a grandson of Joseph Richards and son of Phineas Richards. He was born in Richmond on Apr. 2, 1821. At age 13 he attended the Lennox Academy, 5 miles east of Richmond. In the summer of 1836 Joseph Smith and Brigham Young came from Kirtland to Richmond. As a result of their labors, Willard, Levi, and Phineas were soon baptized in the **pool.** Franklin left Richmond to go to Far West, MO, on Oct. 22, 1838. Ten years later Franklin D. Richards was ordained an **Apostle** by Heber C. Kimball. He completed several missions to England, where he served as president of the mission more than once. He was President of the Quorum of the Twelve for about a year before his death in 1899 (BiE 1:53, 115–21).

■ **Canaan, NY—Boyhood Home of Parley P. and Orson Pratt**

Located over the New York border and 5 miles NW of Richmond is Canaan, home of Parley P. and Orson Pratt during their youth. Thankful Halsey, Parley's wife, also came from Canaan (APPP 19–30).

■ **Pittsfield—Birthplace of Bishop Edward Partridge**

*Edward Partridge*

Pittsfield is the largest city in the extreme west end of Massachusetts. It is located where U.S. 7 and 20 meet.

Here **Edward Partridge** was born to William and Jemima Partridge on Aug. 27, 1793. At the age of 20, Edward became disgusted with the religious world but maintained his faith in God and the scriptures. In 1828 he became a convert to the Campbellite faith and was baptized at Mentor by Sidney Rigdon. Partridge was converted to the LDS Church when Oliver Cowdery and Parley P. Pratt came to the Kirtland area in 1830. He then went to New York with Sidney Rigdon, where Joseph Smith baptized him in the Seneca River. Writing of Partridge, Joseph Smith said, "he was a pattern of piety." Right after Partridge's baptism, the Lord gave a special revelation through Joseph Smith to Edward (D&C 36) encouraging him in the work of God. Partridge was called to be the **first bishop** in the Church, because, said the Lord, "his heart is pure before me, for he is like Nathanael of old, in whom there is no guile" (D&C 41:11).

Edward Partridge was the bishop in Zion, Jackson Co., MO, where he was tarred and feathered in the public square of Independence on July 20, 1833, for being a Mormon who would not leave the county. Bishop Partridge died in Nauvoo, IL, on May 27, 1840 at age 46 (BiE 1:218–22).

Fifteen miles north of Pittsfield is **Adams Township** where **Alpheus Gifford** was born Aug. 29, 1793 (HC 4:484).

Four miles west of Pittsfield on U.S. 20 is the restored **Hancock Shaker Village.**

# Connecticut

■ AVON

**Wilford Woodruff** came here in Apr. 1827 to live with his aunt, **Helen Wheeler,** and "took her flour mill . . . on shares and worked it for three years" (WW 9, 23).

Wilford and **Jonathan Hale** later preached here in 1837. Bro. Woodruff baptized his uncle, **Ozem Woodruff,** his aunt, **Hannah,** and their son, **John,** on June 12, 1837, in Avon (WW 73).

■ BOLTON

**Jared Carter** and **John F. Boynton** attended a special conference here in July or Aug. 1834. Two were baptized "and many others had their minds to enquire into the truth" (EMS Sept. 1834).

■ CANAAN

**Brigham** and **Joseph Young** preached here in 1836 and baptized four persons (M&A Nov. 1836, p. 408). **Wilford Woodruff** and **Jonathan Hale** visited the church here in 1837 (EJ Oct. 1837, p. 1).

■ CANTON

**Wilford Woodruff** and **Jonathan Hale** taught the gospel here in June 1837 (EJ Oct. 1837, p. 1).

■ COLEBROOK

**Wilford Woodruff** and **Jonathan Hale** taught the gospel here in June 1837 (EJ Oct. 1837, p. 1).

■ COLLINSVILLE

In May 1830 **Wilford Woodruff** was employed to run the flour mill of Mr. **Samuel Collins,** and after a short time of boarding with "about thirty young men" took up residence with the family of

**Dudley D. Sackett** (WW 27–28). In 1837 Wilford and **Jonathan Hale** preached here (EJ Oct. 1837, p. 1).

■ **DEEP RIVER**

**Aurelia Spencer Rogers,** first president of the Primary organization (1878), was born here Oct. 4, 1834, to **Orson Spencer** and **Catherine Curtis** (BiE 3:224).

■ **DERBY**

**Orson Hyde,** an Apostle from 1835 to 1878, came to live here with the **Nathan Wheeler** family following the death of his mother, **Sally,** in 1812. In 1819, when Orson was 14, they moved to Kirtland, OH (BiE 1:80).

**Elizabeth Ann Smith,** who became the wife of Newel K. Whitney, was born here Dec. 26, 1800.

■ **EAST HADDAM**

**Lydia Gates Mack,** Joseph Smith's maternal grandmother, was born here Sept. 3, 1732. **Solomon Mack,** Joseph's grandfather, was married to Lydia in the Second Congregational Church here on Jan. 4, 1759 (JSN 164ff).

■ **FAIRFIELD**

**Lyman Wight,** an Apostle from 1841 to 1849, was born here on May 9, 1796 (BiE 93).

■ **FARMINGTON**

**Wilford Woodruff,** fourth President of the Church, was born here Mar. 1, 1807 to **Aphek Woodruff** and **Beulah Thompson.** Wilford assisted his father in the Farmington mills while in his youth and continued to live at home between various jobs until 20 years of age (WW 3, 23).

In July 1837 Woodruff and **Jonathan Hale** preached here (EJ Oct. 1837, p. 1).

In 1838 Woodruff organized a branch here (HiR 95; WW

90–92). Woodruff stopped here while travelling to Nauvoo from Boston on July 22, 1844. He ordained his father a high priest and patriarch, and "sealed him up unto eternal life" (WW 209).

■ **HADDAM**

Members of the Church and their homes were stoned by a mob here in 1836 (M&A Nov. 1836, p. 414).

■ **HARTFORD**

**William** and **Elizabeth Pratt,** ancestors of Apostles **Parley P.** and **Orson Pratt,** were among the first founders of the colony in Hartford in June 1636 (HiR 5:40).

■ **KILLINGWORTH**

**Jared Carter** baptized 3 persons here in June 1834 (EMS Sept. 1834).

■ **MADISON**

**Orson Pratt** baptized 8 people here in 1833. **Jared Carter** visited and baptized one person here in 1834 (EMS Sept. 1834).

■ **NEW HARTFORD**

**Wilford Woodruff** managed Richard B. Cowles's flour mill here in 1832 (DHC 3:337).

■ **NEW HAVEN**

**Horace R. Hotchkiss** of New Haven sold property to the Saints in Nauvoo. Hyrum Smith and Dr. Isaac Galland visited Mr. Hotchkiss in New Haven, but he refused to honor terms of the purchase (HC 4:406–7).

■ **NORFOLK**

**Jared Carter** baptized one person here in 1834 (EMS Sept. 1834).

■ NORWALK

On Jan. 1–2, 1845, sisters of the Norfolk Branch organized a sewing society to furnish traveling elders with clothing (T&S Feb. 15, 1845, p. 807).

■ OLD LYME

**John Mack,** born in Inverness, Scotland, in 1653, was the first of **Lucy Mack Smith's** line to come to America. Eventually he settled in Lyme in 1734. His son, **Ebenezer Mack,** was born here Dec. 8, 1679, and became the pastor of the Second Congregational Church. **Solomon Mack,** son of Ebenezer, was born here Sept. 15, 1732, and was the maternal grandfather of Joseph Smith (CHC 1:17–18). **Salmon Gee,** one of the first seven Presidents of the Seventy from 1837 to 1838, was born here on Oct. 16, 1792 (HJS 1).

■ OXFORD

**Orson Hyde,** Apostle from 1835 to 1878, was born here on Jan. 8, 1805 (HC 1:217; BiE 1:80).

■ SALISBURY

Elders **Orson Hyde** and **Samuel H. Smith** were the first missionaries of the Church in Connecticut. They arrived in Salisbury on June 3, 1832 (CN Oct. 29, 1932, p. 3).

■ SOUTH NORWALK

**Louie Boulton Felt,** first general president of the **Primary Association** of the Church was born here May 5, 1850. She served in this capacity for 45 years (1880–1925). Her husband was Joseph Felt.

■ SUFFIELD

**Fredrick Granger Williams** was born here on Oct. 28, 1787. Fredrick served as second counselor to the Prophet Joseph Smith in the First Presidency from 1833 to 1837 (HC 1:125; BiE 1:51).

■ WATERBURY

**Isaac Hale,** father of **Emma Hale Smith,** was born here on Mar. 21, 1763 (NEW 114).

■ WESTPORT

**Margaret Young Taylor,** wife of **John Taylor,** was born here Apr. 24, 1837 (LJT 495).

# Rhode Island

■ NEWPORT

**Orson Hyde and Samuel H. Smith** were the first known missionaries in Newport. They preached here in July 1832, and baptized two converts. By 1844 the branch had 21 members (CN July 15, 1972, p. 2; EnH 700).

■ PROVIDENCE

In 1830 **Thomas B. Marsh** taught the gospel to **Mary Ann Angell,** who was working in Providence. He left her a Book of Mormon. She was baptized in New York by John P. Greene and moved to Kirtland in 1833. In 1834 Mary Ann became the **wife of Brigham Young.** Brigham Young's first wife, Miriam Angeline Works, had died in 1832 (BYAM 33, 37).

    Elders **Orson Hyde and Samuel H. Smith** preached here in 1832 and escaped a near tar and feathering by a mob (BiE 1:280; OrH 32). By 1834 there were a number of members in Providence (M&A Dec. 1834, pp. 44–45).

    In 1836 **Joseph Smith** and party took a steamer from New York City to Providence on their way to Salem, MA (HC 2:464).

    A **branch of the Church** was organized here on June 7, 1857. In 1876 a grand Sunday School jubilee was held here. The Providence *Morning Star* was a staunch advocate of fair play as far as the Saints were concerned, especially during the persecution of the Saints under the Edmunds-Tucker law (EnH 700).

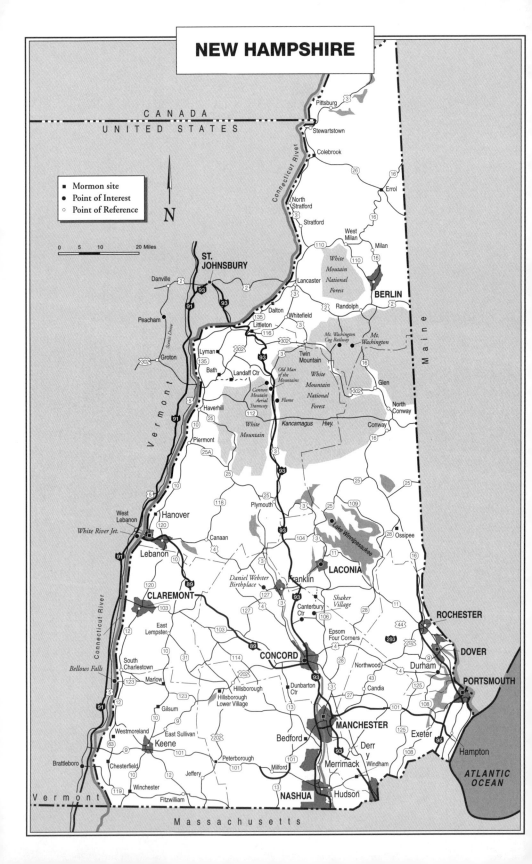

# NEW HAMPSHIRE

## WITH SELECTED SITES IN MAINE

## A. Gary Anderson

NEW HAMPSHIRE, NAMED BY JAMES MASON FOR HIS county in England, became a state in 1776 as one of the original 13. It is known as the Granite State because of its many quarries, but its economic development has been supported also by sheep raising, poultry, dairy and vegetable farming and manufacturing.

More than 80 percent of New Hampshire remains under forest cover, including the White Mountains, which occupy an area of more than 1,200 square miles in the northern half of the state. East of the Rockies the White Mountains are exceeded in elevation only by mountains in North Carolina and Tennessee. They provide numerous ski areas and youth camps. The level of the valley ranges from 500 to 1,000 feet, and Mt. Washington towers 5,288 feet above the valley floor (elevation 6,288'). It is this feature that gives the White Mountains such an unusual impressiveness.

Many writers have been attracted to the beauty of New Hampshire's White Mountains, i.e. Nathaniel Hawthorne, Edward Roth, Ralph Waldo Emerson, Henry D. Thoreau, William Ellery Channing, Thornton Wilder, and Robert Frost. Visitors come to see the spectacular fall foliage which peaks about the first week of October.

## Latter-day Saints in New Hampshire

The first Mormon missionaries to visit New Hampshire were Orson Pratt and Lyman E. Johnson. They baptized converts in the area of Bath in Apr. 1832 (EMS v. 1, no. 10, p. 78; JOP Sept. 8, 1833; EnH 574; JH Apr. 27, 1832).

New Hampshire was the home of Joseph Smith's ancestry on both his mother's and father's sides. His mother was born here, and his paternal grandfather, Asael, lived here. In addition to Joseph Smith's ancestry, many early converts and leaders of The Church of Jesus Christ of Latter-day Saints came from New Hampshire.

# Southwest

■ WINCHESTER—**Birthplace of Josiah Stowell**

Located five miles north of the New Hampshire-Massachusetts border on State 10 is the small town of Winchester, where **Josiah Stowell** was born Mar. 22, 1770. He moved from here to South Bainbridge, NY, in the "Big Bend" of the Susquehanna River.

In the fall of 1825 Stowell employed Joseph Smith to help him dig for legendary Spanish treasures in the Harmony, PA, area. Josiah Stowell's interest in Joseph Smith placed the young prophet in a physical position to meet his future bride, Emma Hale. Joseph later translated the Book of Mormon at Harmony, PA. Joseph also received several revelations in that area, including D&C: 3–13 and 24–27 (HC 1:17; CHC 1:81–83; NEW pp. 177–81).

■ CHESTERFIELD—**Birthplace of John Johnson**

Twelve miles north of the New Hampshire-Massachusetts border on State 63 is the very small village of Chesterfield, birthplace of **John Johnson** (Apr. 11, 1778).

During the Kirtland period of Church history, Joseph Smith lived for a year with John Johnson at Hiram, OH (Sept. 1831– Sept. 1832). It was near John Johnson's house that Joseph was tarred and feathered (Mar. 24, 1832).

Fifteen revelations, including the spectacular D&C 76, were received by Joseph Smith while residing at Hiram in the Johnson home.

■ WESTMORELAND—**Home of Thomas B. Marsh and Sally Carlisle Randall**

Five miles north of Chesterfield on State 63 is the village of Westmoreland where **Thomas B. Marsh** lived until he was 14 years of age. He was born in Massachusetts. Marsh was ordained one of the first Twelve Apostles and was President of the Quorum from 1835 to 1838. He was appointed President pro tem of the Church in Missouri on Feb. 5, 1838, and was excommunicated on Mar. 17, 1839, for apostasy. He was rebaptized July 16, 1857, moved to Utah, and died in full fellowship in 1866 (BiE 1:74–76). **Sally Carlisle Randall** was born in Westmoreland in 1805. She converted to the Church and joined the Saints in Nauvoo. Through her letters one can appreciate the conditions in Nauvoo during the mobbings, the death of Joseph Smith, and the move to the West (WV 134–46).

### ■ PETERBOROUGH—"Our Town"

Eighteen miles north of the New Hampshire-Massachusetts border on U.S. 202, along the banks of the Contoocook River, is the small town of Peterborough. It is dubbed "Our Town" because Thornton Wilder wrote the Pulitzer prize-winning play by that name while living here. The Mormons played a significant role in the history of Peterborough. The town's written history devotes one full chapter to the Mormons. Although visited by missionaries in 1832, it wasn't until 1841 when **Eli P. Maginn** came to Peterborough that the Mormons had enough success to organize a branch of the Church here. Elder Maginn was an English convert who was said to have been a lively, fascinating speaker. He had great knowledge of the Bible. He attracted crowds from far and near to hear him preach. He wasn't allowed to use any of the local churches for his preaching, so he held his meetings in a little hall on the third floor of the **Goodrich Block** at 63–65 Main Street (now a parking lot). Many were converted to Mormonism.

After Elder Maginn's successful experience, many well-known Mormon Elders preached in Peterborough, including Julian Moses, Erastus Snow, Parley P. Pratt, Ormus Bates, Charles A. Adams, Hyrum Smith, Orson Pratt, William Lowe, George A. Smith, and Brigham Young. As many as 230 people were reported to have converted to the Mormon faith during the decade 1840–50 as a result of the meetings held in Peterborough. Some of the converts came from surrounding towns. On July 14, 1844, there were 28 men ordained elders in one day at Peterborough. Solomon Mack II was one of those ordained. Perhaps the three most prominent Mormons who were a part of Peterborough's history were Brigham Young, his wife Naamah Carter, and Jesse C. Little.

**Brigham Young** was in Boston when Joseph Smith was martyred June 27, 1844. On that day Brigham Young felt a heavy depression of spirit come upon him. It was not until July 16, while at Brother Bement's house in Peterborough, that Brigham Young heard a letter read which Brother Livingston had received from Mr. Joseph Powers of Nauvoo. It gave particulars of the martyrdom. Brigham Young said: "The first thing that I thought of was whether Joseph had taken the keys with him from the earth; Brother Orson Pratt sat at my left; we were both leaning back in our chairs. Bringing my hand down on my knee, I said, 'the keys of the Kingdom are right here with the Church'" (CHC 2:413). Brigham left for Lowell immediately, and on the next day (17th) joined fellow members of the Quorum of the Twelve. He was to take Joseph Smith's place and become the second prophet of the Church (HC 7:185; CHC 2:413; JI 6:103).

**Naamah Kendall Jenkins Carter** of Peterborough was baptized into the Church on Apr. 13, 1842. She moved to Nauvoo in March 1845 and married John Saunders Twiss May 30, 1845, with Brigham Young officiating. After her husband's death Sept. 10, 1845, she became Brigham Young's 14th wife.

**Jesse C. Little** had a store in Peterborough for many years. He was born in Belmont, ME, on Sept. 26, 1815, joined the Church in the East and was appointed president of the New England States Mission in 1846. He made arrangements with President James K. Polk for the enrollment of the Mormon Battalion. He left his wife and two children in Peterborough while he journeyed to Utah with the first pioneer company in 1847. He later opened a hotel at the Warm Springs in Salt Lake City. He was a colonel in the Utah Militia and a counselor to Edward Hunter in the Presiding Bishopric (BiE 1:242–43).

■   GILSUM (BOYLE)—Birthplace of Lucy Mack

Gilsum is located in the upper Ashuelot Valley of Cheshire County, on State 10, about 8 miles north of Keene and about 6 miles south of Marlow (HJS 29–30; CHC 1:13, 17–28; JSN 18ff; T&S 5:760; BOM 13–16; HTG 58–59, 123–25, 136–240). The area covered by the township was given the name "Boyle" in 1752. In

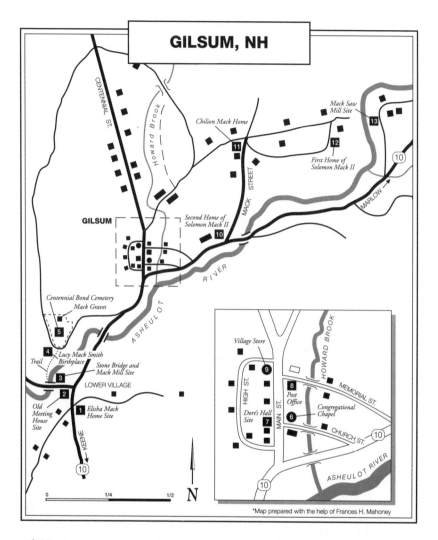

GILSUM, NH

*Map prepared with the help of Frances H. Mahoney

1763 the name was changed to "Gilsum," a compromise name desired by Samuel Gilbert and Clement Sumner.

It was here that **Lucy Mack Smith,** mother of Joseph Smith the Prophet, was born to Solomon and Lydia Mack near the Centennial Bond Cemetery on July 8, 1775. Lucy's youngest brother **Solomon Mack II** was also born in Gilsum.

When entering Gilsum from the south on State 10, the following sites may be visited in order of appearance:

■ **1. ELISHA MACK HOME SITE.** This site is located in "Lower Village" on the east side of State 10 about 1 to 2 blocks SE of the Old Stone

Bridge and Mack Mill site. Elisha Mack and Samuel Mack were older brothers of Solomon Mack I. They helped build the **first dam and bridge** across the Connecticut River near Bellows Falls. The bridge built in 1784–85 connected Walpole, NH, with Rockingham, VT. Elisha Mack was known as Captain Elisha Mack in the Revolutionary War and was the hero of the notorious Keene Raid on May 31, 1779, in which he broke up some Tory bands. **Solomon Mack I** lived for a time in Elisha's house before he moved to Tunbridge, VT.

■  **2. OLD MEETING HOUSE SITE.** Located in "Lower Village" immediately SE of the "Stone Bridge" this site is on a grassy spot just north of a house on the west side of the road.

In 1836 **Joseph Smith Sr.** and his brother **John Smith** visited their relatives in Gilsum to convert them to their new "Mormon" faith.

In 1841 Elders **E. P. Maginn** and **Austin Cowles** held a protracted meeting in the **Old Meeting House.** They received 16 converts from this and the neighboring towns. The **Gilsum Branch** of Latter-day Saints was organized at this time, no doubt in the Old Meeting House. In the years following the branch organization, the meetings were held in Dort's Hall. Annual town meetings were held in the Old Meeting House for many years.

■  **3. STONE BRIDGE, "THE GREAT BRIDGE," AND MACK MILL SITE.** The present Stone Bridge over the Ashuelot River is located in "Lower Village" just NW of the Old Meeting House. It is built in the same place that Elisha and Solomon I built **"The Great Bridge"** in 1776.

The **first gristmill** in Gilsum was built about 1776 on the SE side of the Ashuelot River, just NE of "The Great Bridge," by brothers Elisha and Solomon Mack I. It was in operation for about 75 years. The site of the mill is known as the **Mack Mill site.**

■  **4. LUCY MACK SMITH BIRTHPLACE.** Located directly south of the SW corner of the Centennial Bond Cemetery, about 150′ south of Centennial Street and on the west side of the old road (now a trail) going south from the cemetery, is the birthplace of Lucy Mack Smith. Here lived Solomon I and Lydia Gates in a log cabin (that no longer exists), and here Lucy Mack was born July 8, 1775.

In 1773, Solomon I and Lydia Mack moved from Marlow to Gilsum and lived here 18 years during three different time periods before 1830: (1) 1773–84 (1785–91 in Montague, MA), (2) 1792–99 (1799–1817 in Royalton, VT. During the time Solomon lived in Royalton, the Prophet Joseph Smith was born in a cabin owned by Solomon I near Royalton), and (3) 1818–20. This last period was after Lydia's death in Royalton. Solomon I returned to Gilsum in 1818 and lived

*Lucy Mack Smith Birthplace—the Solomon Mack Home Site, Gilsum, NH. (1973)*

with his son, Solomon II, in NE Gilsum (site #12).

*Lucy Mack Smith, mother of the Prophet Joseph Smith. A steel engraving from a real life sketch by Frederick Piercy, 1853*

Solomon Mack I, grandfather of Joseph Smith, was an adventurous soul. He spent many years as a sea captain. Although he was a moral and honest man, he never considered himself religious. He spent his final years advising people not to spend their life in material pursuits as he had done, but to lay up treasures in heaven by finding the joy of a conversion to Christ.

■ **5. CENTENNIAL BOND CEMETERY.** The Mack family burial site is located near Solomon Mack I's log home site. Solomon I died in Gilsum in 1820 at age 88 and was buried here. Mack family tombstones are located about 465′ north from the road on the south of the cemetery and 200′ east of the road on the west side of the cemetery. The tombstones from south to north belong to Solomon Mack I (Joseph Smith's grandfather), Esther Mack, Amos Mack, Esther (Solomon II's wife), Solomon Mack II, Betsy, and C.

*Solomon Mack I Tombstone, Centennial Bond Cemetery, Gilsum, NH. (1973)*

Alexander Mack. Immediately behind (west of) the Macks' tombstones is a crypt used in the past to store coffins with bodies during
the winter when the ground was frozen too hard to dig.

● **6. CONGREGATIONAL CHAPEL.** Located in the center of the village
on the corner of Main and Church Streets, the Congregational
Chapel was originally built in 1834. It was subsequently owned by
the Methodists, and then, in 1876, the town purchased it for $700
to serve as the first town hall. It is used now for church meetings
by both Congregationalists and Catholics.

■ **7. DORT'S HALL SITE—LDS MEETING HOUSE SITE.** On Main Street,
across from the Congregational Chapel, is where The Church of
Jesus Christ of Latter-day Saints held their meetings from 1842 to
1857. The present building was used as a hotel but is now a home.
Dort's Hall was attached to the rear of the structure. It had a
dance floor on springs, was used for all sorts of meetings, and was
torn down about 1950.

The first Gilsum Branch of the Church was organized about
1841 in the Old Meeting House (Site #2). Shortly after organization, branch meetings were being held in Dort's Hall.

The **first** recorded **branch president** of the Gilsum Branch was
Elder **Charles A. Adams,** Apr. 30, 1843. Chilion Mack was the
clerk. In Aug. 1843, **Jesse C. Little** was sustained as the branch
president. On July 14 Solomon Mack II was ordained an elder in
Peterborough by Brigham Young and Orson Pratt. He served later
as branch president.

On May 26, 1849, the branch was reorganized by Elder Joseph
Grover in the home of Solomon Mack II. Grover became the
branch president, and the branch was named the Cheshire
County Branch. There had been some contention in the branch
over the question of "following the brethren," hence the need of
the reorganization.

President Grover was replaced as branch president on July
21–22, 1849, by Solomon Mack II. The branch was again reorganized
Aug. 21, 1855, by Martin H. and E. M. Pack. Solomon Mack II was
reappointed the president and John Young was appointed the clerk.

In 1857 Elder Wm. H. Branch, a Utah missionary, visited
Gilsum and rebaptized most of the members. This was the period
of the Mormon Reformation of 1856–57. The branch was disorga-
nized after 1857.

Solomon Mack II, his wife, Adaline R., his son Solomon Mack III, and his brother Chilion were all members of the Gilsum Branch at one time. Solomon Mack III made his way to Kansas and intended to join the Saints in Utah, but his family was not willing to go with him, so he returned home. Solomon Mack II was a captain in the militia and served the town of Gilsum as a selectman. Chilion Mack was the first postmaster in Gilsum and held the office for 14 years.

■ **8. THE POST OFFICE.** The Gilsum Post Office is located just north of the Congregational Church on Main Street. The first postmaster of Gilsum was **Chilion Mack,** grandson of Solomon Mack I. Chilion was appointed on Dec. 20, 1828, and held the office for 14 years. Chilion also spent several years in the California mines.

● **9. THE VILLAGE STORE.** Located on the west side of Main Street a little north of the Post Office is the village store.

■ **10. THE SECOND HOME SITE OF SOLOMON MACK II.** Located on Mack Street near State 10, this house was built by Solomon II in 1835. Solomon II took in boarders.

On May 26, 1849, the **branch** of the **Church** in **Gilsum** was **reorganized** in this home. The name was changed to the Cheshire County Branch, and Joseph Grover was sustained as the branch president. On July 21–22, 1849, Solomon Mack II became the branch president. He served in this office nearly continuously until about 1857.

■ **11. CHILION MACK HOME SITE.** Chilion's home was located north of the second home of Solomon Mack II, just west of Mack Street. It was built in 1845. Chilion, grandson of Solomon Mack I, was the first postmaster of Gilsum and served from 1828 to 1842. He was a member of the Church and served as a clerk in the branch.

■ **12. FIRST HOME SITE OF SOLOMON MACK II.** Solomon II built his first home in Gilsum in 1805 in the NE part of the town. This property became known as the "Mack Farm." When **Solomon Mack I** moved to Gilsum in 1818 after his wife Lydia's death in Royalton, VT, he stayed with his son, Solomon II, for two years before he died in 1820.

Solomon II was a captain in the militia and served the town as a selectman. He also served as the branch president at Gilsum. **Solomon III,** also a captain in the militia, occupied Solomon II's home in the 1880s. **Three generations** of Solomon Macks lived in the same home.

■ **13. THE MACK SAWMILL.** Long since gone, the sawmill was located on the east bank of the Ashuelot River just off State 10 in NE Gilsum. It was built by Orlando Mack and his father, Solomon II.

■ MARLOW—**Home of Solomon Mack I (1761–73)**

Six miles northeast of Gilsum, on State 10, is the very small village of Marlow. This was the home of **Solomon Mack I,** maternal grandfather of the Prophet Joseph Smith. Solomon I and his wife, Lydia Gates, left Granville, NY, in 1761 and traveled to the unsettled wilderness of Marlow, NH, to become the first residents of the town which was later organized in 1766. Before this time there was very little settlement in the area by white men because of the Indian threat. With the close of the French and Indian War, the Connecticut River Valley looked promising to former militiamen, including Solomon I. His wife, Lydia Gates, taught the children, as there were no schools close enough to attend. Solomon I built two homes adjacent to the present Marlow cemetery, and four of his children were born here: Louisa (ca. 1761), Lovina (ca. 1762), Jason (ca.

1764), and Stephen (1766). Other children in the family were Lydia, Lucy, Daniel, and Solomon II. Solomon Mack I was elected game warden of Marlow in 1767. After 10 years in Marlow, he moved his family to Gilsum in 1773, where they lived three different times for a total of 18 years.

*Home of Solomon and Lydia Mack, Marlow, NH. (1973)*

The Mack name became a very prominent and respected name in Marlow, not only because of Solomon Mack I, but also because of his brother Elisha and relatives John, Zopher, and Silas Mack. A Revolutionary War statue in the town

*Mack Mountain and Solomon Mack's Home Site; about where the tombstone stands, Marlow, NH. (1973)*

square bears the names of Zopher, John, and Silas Mack. A prominent hill behind the village is called **Mack Mountain.** An old mill site also bears the Mack name. Silas Mack was a member of the school board and an active member of the local Baptist church. Silas Mack, Orville Mack, and Daniel Mack are buried in the old **Marlow Cemetery** (HJS 1–31; CHC 1:19; BOM 13–16).

### ■ WEST LEBANON—Home of the Joseph Smith Sr. Family

West Lebanon, where the Mascoma River joins the Connecticut River, is on I-89, ½ mile east of I-91 near White River Junction, VT.

The first settlers arrived in Lebanon in 1762. The St. Francis Indians called the beautiful Connecticut River Valley area "Mascoma." The story is told that during the French and Indian War **Phineas P. Parkhurst** rode on horseback over 20 miles to warn the citizens of Lebanon of the burning and pillaging of Royalton, VT,

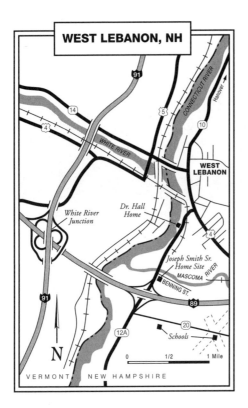

**WEST LEBANON, NH**

CONNECTICUT RIVER

Hanover

91

14

5

4

10

WHITE RIVER

WEST
LEBANON

White River
Junction

Dr. Hall
Home

4

Joseph Smith Sr.
Home Site

MASCOMA RIVER

BENNING ST.

91

89

12A

20

Schools

N

0        1/2        1 Mile

VERMONT    NEW HAMPSHIRE

by the Indians. Parkhurst stopped at the home of **Dr. Hall** in West Lebanon (on the west side of South Main Street [Highway 12 A] 4.4 miles north of the Mascoma River) to have an Indian bullet removed from his side. The house of Dr. Hall is over 200 years old and is still standing. It is numbered 68. Apparently Phineas P. Parkhurst decided to become a doctor after watching Dr. Hall remove the bullet, and it is possible that Dr. Phineas P. Parkhurst was the family physician of the Joseph Smith Sr. family.

**Joseph Smith Sr.** and his family moved to West Lebanon from South Royalton, VT, in 1811 and remained here for about two years. To find the **Joseph Smith Sr. homesite** from I-91 paralleling the Connecticut River, exit at White River Junction and travel east on I-89 ½ mile to State 12 A (Exit 20). Go north on 12 A (a southern extension of West Lebanon's Main Street) about ¹/₁₀ mile

*House Joseph Smith Sr. rented in West Lebanon, NH. Here, in 1813, seven-year-old Joseph Smith Jr. had his leg operated on. (Courtesy of Russell R. Rich; 1967)*

after the exit, to the site of the rented Joseph Smith Sr. house. It was located on the east side of the road ¹/₁₀ mile south of the Mascoma River, on what is now the southeast corner of Benning and Main Streets 1 mile south of the West Lebanon city center. Before the present business building was built, the Joseph Smith Sr. home was torn down (Sept.–Oct. 1967).

*Poverty Lane School, West Lebanon, NH, where Joseph Smith Sr.'s children probably went to school. (1967)*

Joseph Smith was a child six or seven years old when his family moved to West Lebanon. It was here that **Catherine,** ninth of the Smith's eleven children, was born on July 28, 1812. While in Lebanon, **Hyrum** attended Moor's Academy, located on the present Dartmouth College campus, 4 ½ miles from the Smith's rented home. The rest of the school-age children probably attended school a short distance from their home on what is still known as "Poverty Lane" and numbered State 20. It goes east from State 12 A at a point just south of the I-89 West Lebanon exit. Going east on State 20 from State 12 A, the road goes up two steps or levels. On the first step, and on the south side of the road, stood an old schoolhouse where Joseph and other Smiths were probably schooled. Another schoolhouse once stood where the airport runways cross. The Smith children may have gone to school there. The old Turnpike Road went across the south part of the runway.

A plague of **typhus fever** was devastating the whole countryside in 1813, and all the children in the Smith family had it. The popular remedy was a hot bath made of a concoction of hemlock boughs; but since tubs large enough to hold a man were rare, a coffin-like tub of pine boards was carried from house to house. **Sophronia,** Joseph's sister, had been sick for 90 days when the doctors gave her up. The power of prayer saved her.

**Joseph Smith,** a little boy about seven years old, received a pain in his shoulder. Dr. Parker opened the swelled arm and it "discharged freely." The disease then descended into Joseph's left leg. Hyrum, Joseph's older brother, sat with Joseph day and night pressing Joseph's leg to relieve the pain. Doctors Smith, Stone, Perkins, and several students from Dartmouth Medical School wanted to amputate Joseph's leg, but Joseph resisted. Dr. **Nathan Smith,** the leading doctor of the team and founder of Dartmouth Medical School, then did a complicated **surgery** without the benefit of anesthesia, in which he removed pieces of infected bone from Joseph's leg. Joseph received treatment that was generations ahead of current practice and attended by the only physician in the United States who aggressively and successfully operated for osteomyelitis, thereby preventing amputation. Joseph said after the surgery, "I was reduced so very low that my mother could carry me with ease" (BYUS Summer 1970, p. 481). (See also HJS 48–58; BYUS Summer 1970, pp. 480–82, Spring 1977, pp. 319–37, Spring 1981, pp. 131–54; NEW 25–26; BOM 31–32).

■  HANOVER—Home of Dartmouth College

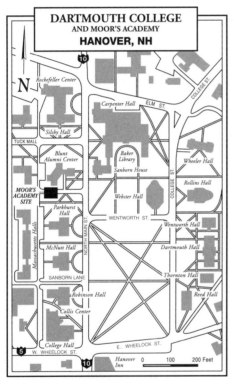

The town of Hanover is located on State 10, 1½ miles north of West Lebanon and ¼ mile east of the Connecticut River.

**Dartmouth College,** chartered by King George III in 1769 to instruct both Indian and English youth, is the predominate feature of Hanover. It is now a privately endowed, coeducational liberal arts school. It has three professional graduate schools: medicine, engineering, and business administration. Eleazar Wheelock founded the college as "Moor's Indian Charity School" about 1750, at Lebanon, CT. He later expanded the school and moved it to Hanover. At Hanover, Moor's Charity School and Dartmouth College were managed by a common board of trustees, and were located adjacent to one another. By 1790 the charity school was known as "Moor's Academy."

**Hyrum Smith,** brother of Joseph Smith, was a 12-year-old student at the Academy about 1811–13. At that time, the school had 30 to 40 students. It was located near the northwest corner of the Dartmouth College green, 100′ north of Wentworth Street and

100′ west of North Main Street, between the Parkhurst Administration Building on the south and the Blunt Alumni Center on the north. The building was sold in 1835, and the school was closed in 1849 (HiH 48). The site was being used as a parking lot in 1995.

*Moor's Charity School, Hanover, NH, on the Dartmouth College campus. Hyrum Smith attended school here. (Courtesy Dartmouth College Library)*

It was from Dartmouth College that **Dr. Nathan Smith** and 10 other doctors and students came to West Lebanon to operate on Joseph Smith's leg, which was apparently infected with osteomyelitis.

**Daniel Webster** and **Robert Frost** were graduates of Dartmouth. **Albert Carrington** was also a graduate at age 22 (class of 1833). Carrington was one of the few college graduates that joined The Church of Jesus Christ of Latter-day Saints during its earliest years. He was a member of the original pioneer company of 1847 and spent more than 20 years as a clerk and assistant to Brigham Young. He also served as an **Apostle** from 1870 to 1885. He died as a member of the Church in 1889 (DHS 1:12; CHC 1:29; BiE 1:126; NEW 25–26; BOM 31–32).

## Northwest

■ **BATH—First Mormon Center in New Hampshire, 1832**

Bath is a very small community located on U.S. 302, five miles east of the Connecticut River in the northwest of New Hampshire.

In the spring of 1832, **Orson Pratt** and **Lyman E. Johnson,** both of whom later became members of the first Quorum of Twelve in the Church in 1835, were the first missionaries to serve in New Hampshire. Elders **Hyrum** and **Samuel H. Smith,** brothers of the Prophet Joseph, preached in New Hampshire in the latter part of 1832. Lyman E. Johnson baptized **Amasa M. Lyman** near Bath on Apr. 27, 1832, and he was confirmed by Orson Pratt the following day. Lyman was ordained an Apostle in 1842 (BiE 1:96–99). By Jan. 1833, there had been over 20 baptisms in Bath, and on Sept. 8,

1833, Orson Pratt and Lyman Johnson "sealed up" the Church in Bath. Pratt and Johnson spent 26 days in New Hampshire the first time. In addition to Lyman, they baptized **Hazen Aldrich,** who became one of the first seven Presidents of the Seventy (1835–37) (BiE 1:186–87).

**Landaff Center,** four miles east of Bath, was one of 10 branches organized as a part of the Vermont Conference by the Twelve on July 17, 1835. Four members of the Church lived here (HC 2:238; JOP Sept. 8, 1835; EnH 574; JH Apr. 27, 1832; see also EMS v. 1, no. 10, p. 6).

■ LITTLETON AND LYMAN

**Littleton** is located on U.S. 302 about 14 miles northeast of Bath. It is located within a mile of I-93 and has a hydroelectric plant that may be visited.

In the early 1830s Mormon meetings were held in West Littleton at the home of **Phineas Parker.** In nearby **Lyman, Amasa Lyman** was born Mar. 30, 1813. He was baptized near Bath on Apr. 27, 1832, by Orson Pratt (Apostle from 1842 to 1867). In 1835, **Elder Erastus Snow**, then only 17 years of age, raised up a **branch** of the Church at Lyman. Mormon meetings in Lyman were at times held in the house of Parker Stickney on the hill above Young's Pond. Because of this, that locality was called **"Mormon Hill."** The families of James, Phineas, and Zadoc Parker eventually emigrated to Salt Lake City (HC 2:238; EnH 574).

■ DALTON—**First Branch of the Church in New Hampshire**

Twelve miles northeast of Littleton on State 135 is **Dalton,** where the **first branch of the Church in New Hampshire** was organized in July 1833, by Elders **Stephen Burnett** and **Lyman E. Johnson.** The branch had 15 members.

In July 1835, the Quorum of the Twelve held a meeting for the Vermont Conference (comprising the state of Vermont) in St. Johnsbury, 18 miles west of Dalton. They made Dalton (15 members), Littleton (10 members), and Landoff (4 members) parts of the Vermont Conference.

■ Colebrook

**Colebrook** is located about 45 miles NNE of Dalton on U.S. 3. Here **Hazen Aldrich** (who had been baptized by Orson Pratt and Lyman Johnson) baptized four people in 1832. When Jeremiah Willey preached the gospel here in 1842, a spirit of persecution arose.

■ Errol

**Errol,** located 20 miles southeast of Colebrook on State 26, had 20 members of the Church in Aug. 1835 (EnH 574; HC 2:238, 253; HJWI 16–17).

● White Mountain National Forest

Located in the center of New Hamshire are the beautiful White Mountains, which have become a popular outdoor recreation center for tourists. Within the 1,100 square-mile national forest, the visitor may enjoy summer and winter sports and the beauty of nature—especially the fall leaves. The scenic Kancamagus Highway (State 112), one of New England's most beautiful drives, crosses the entire range east to west. Central in this mountain mass is the Presidential Range with 86 peaks. **Mt. Washington,** the highest peak in the northeastern U.S. (6,288'), is the predominant feature. The first **cog railway** in North America (1869), climbs from Crawford Notch on the west side of the peak to its top (3 miles—3 hours). The east side may be climbed by auto beginning at Pinkham Notch (8 miles).

The **Old Man of the Mountain** (Hawthorne's "Great Stone Face"), a natural granite profile of a man's head, is located near Profile Lake on U.S. 3 at Franconia Notch, about nine miles north of North Woodstock. The profile is featured in the state emblem. Near the stone face is **The Flume,** a lovely river gorge 70' deep by 800' long with waterfalls and pools.

**Nathaniel Hawthorne** made use of the White Mountain locale in many of his short stories. His "Great Carbuncle" is associated with the eastern slope of Mt. Washington, where many people are lured in search of this magic and mysterious stone. The region around Mt. Monadnock attracted such writers as Emerson, Thoreau, and Channing. Whittier, Larcom, and Longfellow were also inspired by New Hampshire's beauty. The scene for Thornton Wilder's *Our Town* (1938) was rural New Hampshire; and the noted America poet Robert Frost (1874–1963) lived most of his life in this state.


# Southeast

■ OSSIPEE—**Home of the Progenitors of Church Leaders and Prophets**

Located on State 171, ½ mile east of State 28 and 9 miles northeast of Wolfeboro, which sits at the southeast corner of Lake Winnipesaukee, is the very small village of Ossipee, where sisters **Sarah Ann** and **Hannah Maria Libby** were born May 7, 1818, and June 29, 1828, respectively. In Nauvoo both of these girls were given to **George A. Smith,** nephew of Joseph Smith, as plural wives by George's first wife, Bathsheba Smith. George A. Smith later became Church Historian (1854–71) and counselor to President Brigham Young (1868–75). Sarah Ann Libby gave birth to **John Henry Smith** on Sept. 18, 1848, in Iowa, and died later in Salt Lake City. Sarah Ann's sister Hannah Maria raised young John Henry Smith in Provo, UT, where Hannah had moved in 1852. John Henry Smith married Sarah Farr, daughter of Lorin Farr, in 1866. **George Albert Smith,** future president of the Church (1945–51), was born of this marriage on Apr. 4, 1870. **John Henry Smith** became an **Apostle** at age 32 and later was a counselor in the First Presidency to Joseph F. Smith (1910–11) (BiE 1:141–44; BOK 125–200).


● LAKE WINNIPESAUKEE AND LACONIA

New Hampshire has 1,300 lakes within its borders, and the Lakes District proper centers around Lake Winnipesaukee located in the mid-eastern part of the state, 40 or 50 miles north of Concord. It is a deep body of water about 22 by 10 miles in size. It contains 274 wooded islands. It was popularized as the setting of the movie *On Golden Pond.* Laconia, site of the World Sled Dog Championships each February, is the chief town on the lake.


● FRANKLIN—**Daniel Webster Birthplace**

Located about 20 miles northwest of Concord and near State 127, four miles SW of Franklin, is the birthplace of **Daniel Webster,** one of the great American orators and politicians. He served as a lawyer before the Supreme Court, congressman, senator, and finally Secretary of State to President Millard Fillmore, friend of the Mormons in Utah. The birthplace consists of a restored two-room cabin with period furnishings and relics.

● CANTERBURY CENTER—Shaker Village

About 15 miles north of Concord and four miles northeast of Canterbury Center is a **Shaker village** and **museum.** Persecution in England drove Ann Lee, founder of the Shaker movement, to America in 1774. The village near Canterbury Center was started in 1793.

● CONCORD AND VICINITY—Mary Baker Eddy Birthplace

Concord, located near the center of the state 35 miles north of the Massachusetts border, replaced Portsmouth as the state capital in 1808.

In Dec. 1842, **Jeremiah Willey** preached the gospel here and baptized one person, Eloza Stevens (HJWI 17).

Four miles south of the city center on state highway 3A near Bow is the birthplace of **Mary Baker Eddy** (1821–1920), founder of Christian Science and the Church of Christ, Scientist (1879). In 1909 she founded the daily paper, *Christian Science Monitor.* The birthplace is marked by a granite pyramid and a grove of pines; the building no longer exists.

■ DUNBARTON CENTER—Home of Asael Smith

Located about 10 miles southwest of Concord on State 13 is Dunbarton Center, home of **Joseph Smith's Grandfather Asael** (1744–1830). After Asael's marriage to Mary Duty, he lived first in Topsfield (1767–72), then in Windham, home of his wife's family (1772–74). He then moved to Dunbarton Center, where he lived with his wife and family for four years (1774–78). Asael apparently did not own land here, and his place of residence is unknown. While living in Dunbarton Center in 1776, Asael took leave of his wife and five children to enlist as a soldier in George Washington's army of the American Revolution under Captain John Nesmith. His company was enrolled to defend New York's northern frontier. His feelings about his country are reflected in this political credo as he counseled his children: "Bless God that you live in a land of liberty, and bear yourselves dutifully and conscionably towards the authority under which you live. See God's providence in the appointment of the Federal Constitution, and hold union and order as a precious jewel" (Address to His Family, JSN 128).

From Dunbarton Center Asael moved to Manchester (1778–85), then back to Topsfield to settle his father's estate. He remained in Topsfield from 1786 to 1791, then moved to Ipswich, MA, for a few months before settling in Tunbridge, VT in Oct. 1791, where he lived for over 20 years. Asael was a farmer and cooper. His last 15–20 years were spent in Stockholm, NY, where he died Oct. 31, 1830, at age 85 (JSN 94; BOM 20).

● **HILLSBOROUGH LOWER VILLAGE—Franklin Pierce Homestead**

Twenty-five miles southwest of Concord and three miles west of Hillsborough on State 31 at Hillsborough Lower Village is the **Franklin Pierce homestead,** home of New Hampshire's only president of the United States (14th, 1853–57). The large two-story frame house where Pierce spent his early years was built in 1804 and has been restored.

■ **MANCHESTER (DERRYFIELD) AND VICINITY—Home of Asael Smith and his son Joseph Smith Sr.**

Located on the banks of the Merrimack River, 20 miles north of the Massachusetts border on U.S. 3 and I-93, is the largest city of New Hampshire, Manchester. It was originally known as Harrytown, then Tyngstown (1735), Derryfield (1751), and finally as Manchester (1810). Industries such as the Amoskeag Manufacturing Company, which once owned the largest cotton mills in the world, make Manchester the industrial center of the state.

**Asael Smith,** grandfather of the Prophet Joseph Smith, came to Derryfield in 1778 from nearby Dunbarton with his wife, Mary Duty, and his six children: Jesse, Priscilla, Joseph, Asael, Mary, and Samuel. He worked as a cooper making barrels during the winter and as a farmer during the summer. He purchased a **100-acre farm** on the Merrimack River on May 27, 1778. This pie-shaped

# MANCHESTER, NH

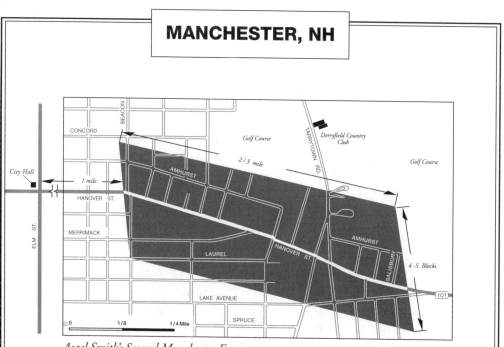

*Asael Smith's Second Manchester Farm*

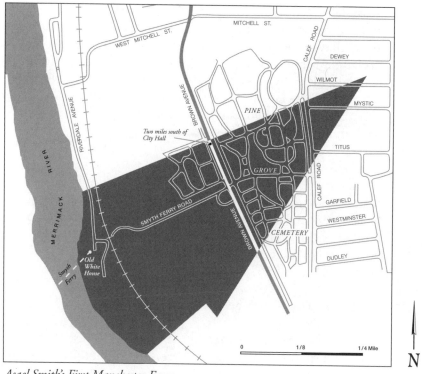

*Asael Smith's First Manchester Farm*

*Information for the maps provided by John T. Mills*

property was located 2 miles directly south of the present city hall and now includes a third of the Pine Grove Cemetery. Brown Avenue bisects the property, and Smyth Ferry Road and Riverdale Road are located within the property. The Merrimack River formed the southwest property line. Asael also acquired another **100-acres** with his brother-in-law, Mark Duty. This rectangular-shaped property was ⅕ mile wide and ⅔ mile long, running east and west from a point one mile east of the present city hall on Hanover Street. This street bisects the property in two equal parts. On an east-west line, the property started on Beacon Street and ran to a point just beyond Salisbury Street. Asael was elected town clerk of Derryfield from 1779 to 1786. He resigned when his father died. He not only regularly signed the minutes of the town meetings but personally recorded the birth dates of most of his large family in the first Derryfield town book. Asael and Mary's children born here were **Silas** (1779); **John** (1781), who became the **fifth Patriarch** to the Church and the president of three stakes: Adam-ondi Ahman, Zarahemla, and Salt Lake (HiR 5:91–92); **Susannah** (1783); and **Stephen** (1785). Asael Smith sold his 100-acre river property to his brother Samuel Smith and returned to Topsfield with his wife and 10 children in 1786 after the death of his father, Samuel. Asael took care of his stepmother and helped liquidate his father's assets and settle the estate. He did this at considerable personal sacrifice to fulfill his obligation to his father. Asael's last child, **Sarah,** was born in Topsfield in 1789 (JSN 89–140; BOM 20–29).

■ BEDFORD—**Birthplace of Mary Bailey**

Four miles southeast of Manchester City Hall on State 101 is Bedford, the birthplace of **Mary Bailey,** first **wife of Samuel H. Smith,** brother of the Prophet Joseph Smith. She was born Dec. 20, 1808, bore four children, and died in Nauvoo, IL, on Jan. 25, 1841 (HJS 339).

■ WINDHAM—**Home of Asael Smith and Mary Duty**

Four miles west of Salem on State 111 (one mile west of Exit #3, I-93) is the village of Windham, where the Prophet Joseph Smith's father and grandfather lived (1772–74).

On May 1, 1772, Asael Smith and his wife, Mary Duty, moved

from Topsfield, MA, to Mary's former hometown of Windham, with their three children: Jesse, Priscilla, and **Joseph Smith Sr.** Three more children, Asahel (1773), Mary (1775), and possibly Samuel (1777), were born at Windham. **Asael (Asahel)** became the fourth **presiding Patriarch** of the Church. While Asael was in the Revolutionary War, his wife Mary probably left her Dunbarton home, especially at child-bearing time, and sought the aid of her parents, Moses Duty and Mary Palmer Duty, who lived in Windham. From Windham, Asael moved his family to Dunbarton, NH, on Apr. 15, 1774 (JSN 92, 191–92; CHC 1:5–13).

■ **PORTSMOUTH—Birthplace of William Harrison Folsom, Church Architect**

Portsmouth, the state capital of New Hampshire prior to 1808, is located in the southeastern part of the state on the south side of the Piscataqua River where it empties into the Atlantic Ocean. It is on the northernmost point of New Hampshire's 18-mile-long seacoast, on I-95.

Ten acres of Colonial Portsmouth, settled in 1630, have been restored and are known as **Strawberry Banke,** which is built around Puddle Dock, the original port. Prosperity from fishing, shipbuilding (a U.S. naval base stands on Seavey's Island and other islands nearby), and manufacturing during its 250-year history has endowed the city of 30,000 with some of America's finest colonial mansions: **Jackson House** (1664), **Warner House** (1716—the earliest Georgian building in New England), **Moffat-Ladd House** (1763), **Wentworth-Coolidge House** (1760), **John Paul Jones House** (ca. 1759), and the home of **Governor John Langdom** (1785), among others. The **University of New Hampshire** is located 10 miles to the northwest in Durham.

**William Harrison Folsom,** born in Portsmouth on Mar. 25, 1815, was the architect of the famous Salt Lake Tabernacle, Salt Lake Theatre, old Salt Lake City Hall, original ZCMI building, and the St. George and Provo Tabernacles. He was the architect and superintendent of construction of the Gardo House and Manti Temple, and assisted in the design of the Nauvoo, Salt Lake, Logan, and St. George Temples. From 1861 to 1867 Folsom served as Church Architect during Truman Angell's illness. As a boy, William moved to Buffalo, NY, with his parents. He was converted at age 24 and with his family moved to Nauvoo. He died in

Salt Lake City in 1901 at age 86 (HC 6:1–2; UHQ v. 43, no. 3, pp. 240–59).

**Elder Wilford Woodruff** spent a few hours as a missionary in Portsmouth on May 9, 1838 (WW 89). In **Dover,** ten miles northwest of Portsmouth, a branch of the Church existed as early as 1833. Meetings were held in the house of Jonathan Hale. In the spring of 1835 the Twelve held a conference in Dover (M&A 1 Jan. 1835, 64; HJW 4–5).

# Maine

**Orson Hyde** and **Samuel H. Smith,** the first LDS missionaries in Maine, arrived in 1832 (EnH 463).

■ **BANGOR**

In 1837 **Wilford Woodruff** and **James Townsend,** a Mormon convert from southern Maine, introduced the gospel here (BiE 1:21–22).

■ **BATH**

In Oct. 1837 **Wilford Woodruff** and **Jonathan Hale** taught the gospel in Pierce's Hall (EJ v. 1, no. 2, p. 18).

■ **BELFAST**

On Feb. 22, 1838, **Wilford Woodruff** and **James Townsend** stayed at the home of Thomas Teppley and the next day they preached in a schoolhouse (WW 85–86).

■ **BELMONT CORNER**

**Jesse C. Little** was born here Jan. 26, 1815 (BiE 1:242–43).

■ **CAMDEN**

**Wilford Woodruff** and **James Townsend** taught the gospel here in the winter of 1837–38 (EJ 1–3).

- **FARMINGTON**

A conference was held here Aug. 28, 1835 which organized the Saints in Maine as the Maine Conference (EnH 463).

- **FOX ISLANDS**

From Aug. to Oct. 1837, **Wilford Woodruff** and **Jonathan Hale** preached the gospel on two islands: **North Fox Island** (North Haven Island) and **South Fox Island** (Vinalhaven Island). During the winter of 1837–38, **Wilford Woodruff** and his wife, **Phoebe,** served as missionaries on the islands. Two branches were organized. Later, about 100 Saints attempted to gather with **Wilford Woodruff** to Missouri. They stopped in Illinois, however, because of persecution in Missouri (ReS 85–99).

- **HAMPDEN**

During the winter of 1837–38, **Wilford Woodruff** and **James Townsend** preached the gospel here (EJ v. 1, no. 3, p. 35).

- **HOPE**

A conference of the Church was held here Dec. 25, 1841. There were 168 members present (HC 4:484–85).

- **JONESPORT**

In Aug. 1866 a group of 156 people under the direction of **George J. Adams** sailed from here to Palestine (TFo 161–76).

- **NEWRY**

Lucy Smith, plural wife of George A. Smith, was born here on Feb. 9, 1817 (BiE 1:39).

- **NORTHPORT**

In Feb. 1838, **Wilford Woodruff** and **James Townsend** preached the gospel here (WW 86).

■ **PORTLAND**

In Aug. 1837 **Wilford Woodruff** and **Jonathan Hale** booked passage
on a steamer for **Owls Head** enroute to the **Fox Islands. Wilford
Woodruff** learned about the death of Joseph Smith while he was
in Portland in July 1844 (MNE 193).

■ **SACO**

**Arthur Milliken,** who married Lucy Smith, youngest sister of the
Prophet, was born here May 7, 1818. **Samuel Brannan,** who led a
group of Saints to California and later became the first millionaire
in California, was born here on Mar. 6, 1819. **Timothy Smith,** the
first convert in Maine, was baptized here on Oct. 31, 1832. Seven
of the Twelve met here in conference on Aug. 21, 1835 (SB, p. 6;
CN Dec. 10, 1932, p. 3; HC 2:252).

■ **SCARBORO**

On Aug. 8, 1837, **Wilford Woodruff** met for the first time the rela-
tions of his wife, **Phoebe.** Sarah Emma, the first child of **Wilford
Woodruff** and **Phoebe Carter** was born here on July 14, 1838
(WW 93).

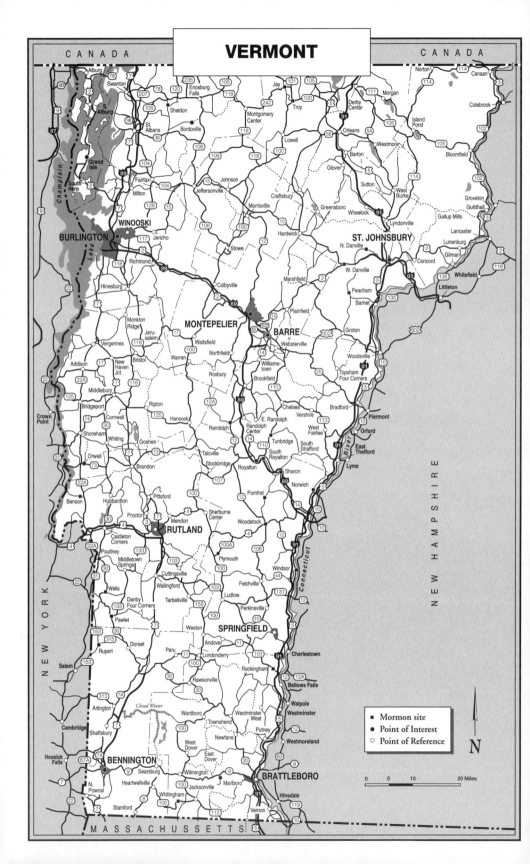

# VERMONT

## Larry E. Dahl

THE GREEN MOUNTAIN STATE, AS VERMONT IS called, was first explored and claimed by a Frenchman, Samuel de Champlain, in 1609. Its name comes from *vert mont,* the French words for "green mountain." Vermont is referred to as the "First Born State," as the first state after the original 13 (1791). This region remained under French control for nearly 150 years after Champlain's initial expedition, and a valley and lake still bear his name.

The establishment of Fort Dummer in 1724 by the English marked the first English settlement in Vermont. Subsequent fighting between the French and the English continued during the French and Indian War until the French relinquished their New England claims to Great Britain in 1763.

The Province of New York received grants of Vermont territory in 1765, but resistance by Ethan Allen and his "Green Mountain Boys" during 1770 and 1771 won Vermont its independence from New York authority. This same group also captured Fort Ticonderoga from the British in 1775 during the Revolutionary War. Vermont became an independent republic on July 8, 1777, and on Mar. 4, 1791, Vermont became the 14th state of the United States—the first to be admitted under the Constitution.

In the War of 1812 Vermont volunteers initially fought the British in numerous battles, but subsequently stopped participating because trade with British-controlled Canada was vital to the state's economy. Fearing economic hardships, many people left the state for better prospects in the Midwest. The opening of the Champlain Canal in 1823 helped offset this challenge by allowing for direct trade with New York City. Wool became Vermont's primary export.

During the Civil War nearly 34,000 Vermonteers served with

Union forces, and the northernmost land action of the war occurred here in 1864 when 22 Confederate soldiers raided banks in St. Albans and fled to Canada. After the war, many inhabitants left the state for factories in the larger cities or for better farmland, and only lumber and dairy industries survived up to the time of the Great Depression. As was the case with many New England states, manufacturing gradually replaced agriculture as Vermont's chief economic activity.

Between the mid-1800s and the mid-1900s, Vermont voters chose only Republicans in presidential and gubernatorial elections. They also chose Republicans in all elections for the U.S. Senate and House of Representatives. No other state has voted so many times in a row for major candidates of the same party. Two Vermont Republicans, Chester Arthur and Calvin Coolidge, became presidents of the United States.

Vermont is not only famous for its green mountains, but also for its forests, marble, granite, and maple syrup. The state's varied geography offers a number of recreational activities. Visitors can enjoy summer boating and fishing, autumn leaves, or winter skiing at one of many resorts. Vermont's quiet towns and villages are also popular tourist attractions (WBE).

## Latter-day Saints in Vermont

To Latter-day Saints Vermont is known as the birthplace of the **Prophet Joseph Smith.** Joseph was born in Sharon township, Windsor County, on December 23, 1805, and lived in various other townships in this state until his family moved to Palmyra, NY, in 1816. Seven of Joseph's nine brothers and sisters were also born in Vermont (CHFT 15, 21).

Several other early Mormon leaders were also born in Vermont, including **Brigham Young,** who as successor to Joseph Smith led the Saints to Utah in 1847 (EnM 4:1601, 1605). **Oliver Cowdery,** scribe to the Prophet, one of the Three Witnesses of the Book of Mormon and Assistant President of the Church, was born in the township of Wells (BOM 96), while **Heber C. Kimball,** a member of the Quorum of the Twelve, was born in Sheldon (TrG 6). Other leaders born in Vermont include Luke S. Johnson, Lyman E. Johnson, Wm. Smith, Erastus Snow, Albert Carrington, Apostles; Zera Pulsipher and Jacob Gates, First Quorum of Seventy; Newel K. Whitney, Presiding Bishop; George W. Robinson, Church Historian; Hiram Page and Samuel Smith, Witnesses of the Book of Mormon plates; and William Marks, Nauvoo Stake President.

Vermont's historical sites associated with the Joseph Smith family are primarily in and near the Connecticut River Valley in the vicinity of White River Junction. Interstate Highways 89 and 95 intersect in this area. The Connecticut River serves as a natural boundary between Vermont and New Hampshire and the valleys created by it provided early settlers with rich farming land. Joseph Smith's ancestors were among the first to settle and farm this beautiful area.

**Jared Carter** was the first Latter-day Saint to introduce the gospel in the state of Vermont (1831). He met with great success, and baptized 27 converts in Benson, and organized a branch here. In 1832 Jared's brother **Simeon Carter** helped Jared in the missionary effort, and by the end of the year there were over 100 members in Vermont (EnH 911). When the Saints of Nauvoo went west in 1846 most of the Vermont Saints went with them leaving very few Mormons in Vermont. In the text below, places important in the history of the Church are listed in a south-to-north geographic order for the eastern half of the state and a north-to-south geographic order for the western half.

■ **WHITINGHAM—Birthplace of Brigham Young**

Whitingham, named after Nathan Whiting, was known as Sadawaga until 1882. It is located about four miles north of the Vermont-Massachusetts border on State 100, near the southern end of Harriman Reservoir, 3½ miles west of Jacksonville. Places of Mormon interest include the following:

**1. "NEW" WHITINGHAM VILLAGE CENTER.** The **"New" Whitingham Village Center** has the typical post office, general store, and church. Diagonally across the road (State 100) from the church is a **sign** commemorating the birthplace of **Brigham Young.** There was no village center in Whitingham when **John Young's** 51½ acres included the current "new" village property. The first village center was built on Town Hill after the Youngs moved to New York in 1804.

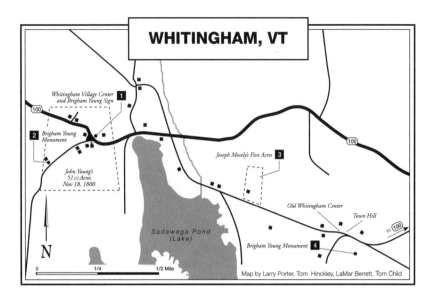

**WHITINGHAM, VT**

Whitingham Village Center and Brigham Young Sign **1**

Brigham Young Monument **2**

John Young's 51 1/2 Acres Nov 18, 1800

Joseph Mosely's Five Acres **3**

Old Whitingham Center

Town Hill

to 100

**N**

Sadawaga Pond (Lake)

Brigham Young Monument **4**

0          1/4          1/2 Mile

Map by Larry Porter, Tom Hinckley, LaMar Berrett, Tom Child

## 2. JOHN YOUNG'S 51½-ACRE FARM AND BRIGHAM YOUNG'S BIRTH-PLACE AND MONUMENT.

In January 1801 **John Young,** father of **Brigham Young,** moved 80 miles NW from Hopkinton, MA, to Whitingham, VT, follow-ing his service in the Revo-lutionary War (under General George Washing-ton) and his marriage to **Abigail (Nabby) Howe.** In Whitingham he pur-chased **51½ acres of land** from his brother-in-law **Joseph Mosely** for $100 (ReS 68), only to sell it back to him for the

*Birthplace of Brigham Young, Whitingham, VT.*

same price less than two years later. After the sale John did, how-ever, remain in this area and open new farms. It is of interest that the center of "new" Whitingham Village is located within John's 51½ acres, including the general store, post office, and church (see map).

In less than five months after their move to Whitingham, the future prophet, **Brigham Young,** was born June 1, 1801. Although the exact location of John Young's cabin where Brigham Young would have been born is not known, someone, prior to 1900,

*President Brigham Young. From a Piercy sketch, 1853.*

placed a stone memorial on a site at the top of Brigham Young Hill, also known as Stimpson Hill, 0.2 miles SW of the church on Stimpson Hill Road (Town Road 33). There is currently a home on the site, and the small stone marker is in the front yard. The inscription on the marker reads: "Brigham Young, born on this spot 1801, a man of much courage and superb equipment." Brigham was John and Nabby's 9th child. In the spring of 1804, the Young family moved to New York state, where Brigham joined the Church in 1832. In Feb. 1835 he was ordained a member of the original Quorum of the Twelve Apostles. Following the death of the Prophet Joseph Smith in 1844, Brigham Young presided over the Church as President of the Twelve Apostles until 1847, when he was sustained as President of the Church, and reorganized the First Presidency. He led the Saints west to present-day Utah, where he founded Salt Lake City and lived there until his death in 1877. A statue of Brigham Young is located in the National Capitol Building, Washington, D.C.

**3. JOSEPH MOSELY'S ORIGINAL FIVE ACRES.** One strain of local tradition suggests that **Joseph Mosely's original five acres** of land in Fitches Grant, Lot 22, was the place of Brigham Young's birth. This acreage is located .7 miles SE of Whitingham Village Center on the north side of Town Hill Road (No. 5). Mosely was John Young's brother-in-law. The most recent careful analysis of the records, however, points to Brigham Young Hill, also known as Stimpson Hill, part of John Young's 51½-acre farm, as the most plausible location of Brigham Young's birth (ReS 65–76).

**4. BRIGHAM YOUNG MEMORIAL MONUMENT.** A 12-foot-high granite monument was placed by descendants of Brigham Young in the Town Hill Memorial Park near the location of the "old" village of Whitingham, which developed after John Young's family moved to New York. It is 1¼ miles SE of the current "new" Whitingham Village, ½ mile east of Sadawaga Lake, in an open field about 350′ south of Town Road 5.

The **monument** was dedicated here on May 28, 1950, by **President George Albert Smith.** The following is an excerpt from his prayer: "We are here now to present this monument of granite, the native granite of this great state, that which President Brigham Young himself undoubtedly would choose if he were here, and, Heavenly Father, we pray that thy Spirit may remain here that those who come to read the inscription on the monument may realize that thou art the Father of us all and that he whom we are gathered to honor was great enough to assume his responsibilities and carry a tremendous load during his long life" (ERA Sept. 1950, p. 693).

■ MARLBORO—**Birthplace of Newel K. Whitney and Newel Knight**

Marlboro is located about 10 miles west of Brattleboro and about ½ mile south of State 9.

*Newel K. Whitney (Courtesy of USHS)*

**Newel K. Whitney** was born here Feb. 5, 1795 (HC 1:145). He became the second bishop of the Church in 1831 (DCE 633–34), and 16 years later became the Presiding Bishop of the Church, in which position he served until his death in 1850. **Newel Knight,** a leader of the Church in Colesville, NY, was born here on Sept. 13, 1800 (ANK 46). He was a close friend of the **Prophet Joseph Smith.** What is referred to as the first miracle in the Church was performed on Brother Knight at Colesville, NY, in Apr. 1830, when the Prophet "cast out a devil from him" (HC 1:82–83). He died at Ponca, NE, in Jan. 1847 (BiE 2:775). Newel's son, Jesse, erected a monument to his father in Niobrara, NE, near the Ponca site (TAMF 178).

The **Congregational Church** in Marlboro dates to 1819, and **Marlboro College** dates to 1947.

■ ROCKINGHAM

Rockingham is located 8 to 9 miles north of Bellows Falls on State 103 near the Vermont-New Hampshire border, nearly 2 miles west of I-91.

**Shadrach Roundy,** a prominent leader in Kirtland and Nauvoo, was born here on Jan. 1, 1789 (FWR 285). **Zera Pulsipher,** one of the

*Shadrach Roundy*       *Zera Pulsipher*

Presidents of the Seventy from 1838 to 1862, was born here on June 14, 1789 (DCE 448). As a missionary in the Eastern States, Pulsipher baptized the future Church President Wilford Woodruff (BiE 1:194).

■ **WINDSOR**

Windsor is located 14 miles south of White River Junction on U.S. 5 and the Connecticut River, a mile east of I-91. Windsor was the scene of the convention where the constitution was written for the state of Vermont. Here Vermont declared itself an independent republic, New Connecticut, in 1777. The tavern where the convention took place is known as the **Old Constitution House,** or the "Birthplace of Vermont," and is located on the main street leading north out of the city. It is open to the public. Windsor was an important center for the manufacturing of guns in the 19th century.

**Solomon Mack's** autobiography, *A Narrative of the Life of Solomon Mack,* was printed here in 1811 (CHFT 19). Solomon, almost 80 years old, probably rode the 35 miles to Windsor from Sharon to arrange for the printing of the pamphlet.

● **PLYMOUTH**

Plymouth is located about 15 miles directly SE of Rutland on State 100A and about 1 mile east of its junction with State 100.

This small town gained renown as the **birthplace of Calvin Coolidge,** the 30th president of the United States, who was here on Aug. 3, 1923, when he heard the news of President Harding's death. His father, a notary public, administered the oath of office to him in the parlor by the light of a kerosene lamp. Visitors can see the **President Coolidge homestead** and explore seven restored buildings, including his home, his birthplace, a church, and a store. Coolidge is buried in the village cemetery just outside of town.

At the foot of Mt. Tom are the famous Plymouth Limestone Caves.

■ WOODSTOCK

Woodstock lies at the junction of U.S. 4 and State 106 about 10 miles due west of White River Junction.

In the winter of 1843, a **branch of the church** was organized here by **William Hyde.** Thirty-five people were baptized. William Hyde, son of Heman and Polly Hyde, was baptized in 1834. He marched to California with the Mormon Battalion in 1846 and was a principal founder of the community of Hyde Park in Cache Valley, UT. He was a bishop, judge, patriarch, the husband of five wives, and father of 25 children (BiE 1:759–63; AWH 11).

At the time of the martyrdom of the Prophet Joseph Smith, June 27, 1844, Elders Erastus Snow and William Hyde were laboring in the vicinity of Woodstock. Immediately upon hearing of the tragedy in Carthage, they returned to Nauvoo, IL (EnH 911).

■ POMFRET

Pomfret is located seven miles SW of Sharon.

Several children of **John** and **Elsa Johnson** were born here. **Luke S. Johnson,** who was one of the Twelve Apostles from 1835 to 1838, was born here on Nov. 3, 1807 (CHFT 617–18). **Lyman Eugene Johnson,** also a member of the Quorum of the Twelve Apostles from 1835 to 1838, was born here on Oct. 24, 1811 (BiE 1:91). **Nancy Marinda Johnson,** wife of **Orson Hyde,** was born here on June 28, 1815 (OrH 53).

*Luke S. Johnson*

■ NORWICH

Norwich is located on U.S. 5 near the Vermont-New Hampshire border, just west of I-91 and across the Connecticut River from Hanover, NH. (From the SW corner of the Dartmouth College campus in Hanover, go west on State 10A across the Connecticut River to U.S. 5, then north ½ mile to Norwich Village Green.)

Norwich is the last place the Smith family lived in Vermont before they left for New York. **Joseph Smith Sr.** moved his family from West Lebanon, NH, to Norwich in 1813 (EAR 11, 24). He rented a farm from **Squire Constant Murdock** and lived here with his family for about three years (1813–16). Tax records for 1813

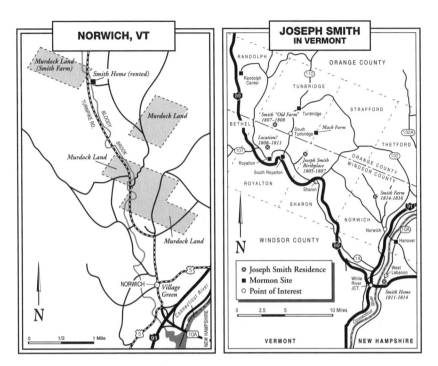

show that Constant Murdock owned three farms, and possibly part of a fourth, in Norwich. Probate records of 1827 and 1828 list three of the farms as the "home farm" (170 acres), the "Hill farm" (60 acres), and the "Smith farm" (140 acres). Although not conclusive, local tradition and an examination of the tax and probate records point to the "Smith farm" as the one Joseph Smith Sr.

*Squire Murdock House and Farm, Norwich, VT, which Joseph Smith Sr. rented. (Photo by George E. Anderson, 1908; courtesy of LDSCA)*

rented—but not because of the name attached to it. It was called the "Smith farm" probably because Squire Murdock purchased that farm from a man named Phillip Smith on Sept. 10, 1810, three years before Joseph Smith Sr. arrived in Norwich.[1]

To get to the Smith farm from White River Junction, start at the Town Square, or Norwich Village Green, with its white church, go due north on Main Street for ³⁄₄ mile, then turn NW (left) onto Turnpike Rd. Go 2 ³⁄₄ miles to the large two-story home of Squire Murdock on the north side of a road that turns east, or right, and goes in front of the home. The house is about ½ block east of Turnpike Rd. (see map). Though the home has been restored and remodeled by new owners, the front of the house has not changed much (GMH 3). According to tradition this is the home and adjoining farm (west of Turnpike Road, see map) that Joseph Smith Sr. rented for about three years (1813–16).

While the Smiths were at Norwich, **Joseph Jr.** was on crutches most of the time, recovering from his 1812 leg operation.

**Don Carlos Smith** was born here on Mar. 25, 1816 (CHFT 21). He died Aug. 7, 1841 at the age of 26 in Nauvoo, IL (MOC 39:759). The year of 1816 was the historical "year without a summer." Snow fell in June. The year was called "Eighteen Hundred and Froze to Death" in Vermont history (SA June 1979, p. 134). For Joseph Smith Sr. this was the last of three successive years of crop failures. He decided he would move about 300 miles to the west like many others were doing, and start over in the farming business. Crop failures caused the Smith family to be heavily indebted, so much so that they were "warned out of town" by local authorities (ReSNY 20). Father Smith left for New York (1816) to investigate the purchase of land there, and soon sent word to his wife to begin her journey to Palmyra, NY with the children (BOM 40–41). Before they left, however, she had troubles with creditors and was forced to sell most of her possessions to pay them. As they began the journey, Lucy's mother, Lydia, was injured when a wagon overturned. Lydia remained in Royalton while Lucy and the children continued the move to New York (HJS 60–62). Lydia died in Royalton two years later.

---

[1] Dr. LaMar E. Garrard and his wife, Agnes, researched the records regarding the location of the farm rented by Joseph Smith Sr. from Squire Murdock. They supplied the author with their research notes as well as copies of Land Deed Records and Tax Records for the village of Norwich (originals located in Norwich City Hall), and probate records of 1827 and 1828 (originals located in Windsor County Court House in Woodstock, VT).

# ■ Sharon Township

In the New England States, the words "town" and "township" are used interchangeably. A "township" is a geographical division of a county, and has cities or villages within its boundaries. Joseph Smith the Prophet was born in the "township" of Sharon, but not in the "village" of Sharon.

The "village" of Sharon is located 13 miles NW of White River Junction on State 14. If traveling east or west on I-89, you will note an exit at the Sharon village.

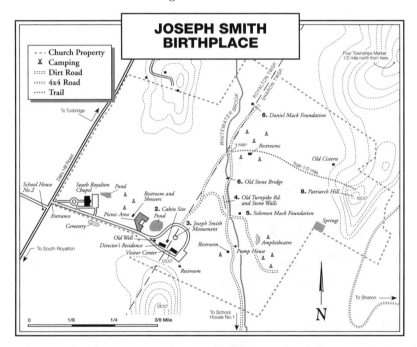

## ■ *Joseph Smith Memorial—Birthplace of the Prophet Joseph Smith*

To get to the Joseph Smith Memorial exit I-89 at Sharon, then go NW on State 14 four miles; then turn right (NE) on Dairy Hill Road. Go two miles to the entrance of the Joseph Smith Memorial.

In 1804 **Solomon Mack** purchased a 100-acre farm 3 miles NW of Sharon Village. The Royalton-Sharon township line divided the farm, with most of it being in the Sharon Township and a small part in the Royalton Township. Solomon paid $800 for the farm, which came with a $441 mortgage he assumed (STR 5:313).

Solomon rented his cabin and 68 acres of the farm to **Joseph Smith Sr.** and his wife, **Lucy,** when they moved from Royalton in 1804. Apparently Solomon and Lydia moved out of their **log cabin** so Joseph and Lucy could move in. Ebenezer Dewey's farm adjoined Solomon's farm in Sharon, so Ebenezer and Solomon knew each other as neighbors. Benjamin Cole Latham signed an affidavit Nov. 14, 1905, in which he said he "heard the elder Dewey [Ebenezer] say that Mack lived there in the house that then stood upon these foundations [of the Prophet's birthplace] both before and after Joseph Smith lived in it" (JSN 176). The fact that Solomon purchased 100 acres at Tunbridge in 1806 adds credence to Latham's affidavit.

*The Prophet Joseph Smith*
*(Courtesy of RLDSLA)*

On Dec. 23, 1805, **Joseph Smith Jr.** was born in the **log cabin.** The future prophet was named Joseph after his father, even though he was the fifth child and third son of Joseph and Lucy. It was an American custom to name the firstborn son after his father, but the prophecy of Joseph of old was fulfilled, and the third son, Joseph, received his father's name (2 Ne. 3:14–15).

The Joseph Smith Sr. family lived on the farm for three years until 1807, when they moved to nearby Royalton, then to Lebanon, NH. While on the Solomon Mack farm, **Joseph Smith Sr.** both **farmed** and **taught school.** It is not known where the school was located, but two possible sites are promoted by tradition. One is on the Turnpike Road which goes north up Whitewater Brook from State 14 at a point 1 ½ miles west of Sharon Village center. A mile north up the Turnpike Road toward the Joseph Smith Monument is a fork in the road, and on the right of the fork is an old schoolhouse, **traditional site no. 1.** It is 1.35 miles from Joseph Smith's birthplace. **Traditional site no. 2** is a schoolhouse remodeled into a home and located on the west side of Dairy Hill Rd., SW across the road from the entrance to the Joseph Smith birthplace property (see map). It is ³/₈ mile from Joseph's birthplace. Both schoolhouses are now private homes.

After the Joseph Smith Sr. family moved from Solomon's Sharon farm in 1807, Solomon moved back from his 100-acre Tunbridge farm (he had purchased this farm from his son Daniel on May 3, 1806 [TTR 3:380]) to his Sharon farm, where he lived four years before he sold it in 1811 to Daniel

*Old School, Sharon, VT, where Joseph Smith Sr. may have taught. Traditional Site No. 2 (1972)*

*Old School, Royalton, VT, where Joseph Smith Sr. may have taught. Traditional Site No. 1 (ca. 1950)*

Gilbert (STR 6:99, 386, 459). Solomon then moved to Tunbridge again, and in 1818, after his wife Lydia's death, he lived in Gilsum, NH, with his son Solomon Jr. until his death on Aug. 23, 1820, at age 88 (JSN 25). He is buried in Gilsum. In summary, Solomon lived on his Sharon farm twice: 1804–5 and 1807–11. He also lived on his Tunbridge farm twice: 1805–7 and 1811–18.

In 1905 the Church bought Solomon's 100-acre Sharon farm plus some adjoining lands totaling 283 acres (see map).

*Junius F. Wells
(Courtesy of LDSCA)*

The purchase was made for the Church by **Junius F. Wells,** originator of the concept to commemorate the centennial of the Prophet's birth by erecting the monument (ERA Feb. 1906, p. 309). Building the **Memorial Cottage** and erecting the **granite monument** was also under the direction of Junius F. Wells, son of Daniel H. Wells. The cost of land and monument was $30,000. Junius was the organizer of the YMMIA (1875) and he established the YMMIA periodical, *The Contributor,* in

*Memorial Cottage and Monument, Sharon, VT. View to the NW.*
*(Photo by George E. Anderson, 1907; courtesy of LDSCA)*

1879. He was the editor for 13 years. In 1921 he served as Assistant Church Historian (BiE 4:249).

Historian T. Edgar Lyon indicated that the purchase of Solomon's farm and the erection of the Joseph Smith Monument "was the beginning of the Church's efforts to identify and appropriately designate sites in the East which related to important events in the restoration of the gospel and the founding and development of the Church" (BYUS Spring 1969, p. 342). Places to visit at the Joseph Smith Memorial include the following:

**1. VISITORS CENTER AND THE HEARTHSTONE.** To commemorate the 100th anniversary of the Prophet Joseph Smith's birth, the

*Joseph Smith Monument and Visitors Center, Sharon, VT. (1972)*

Church erected a **granite monument** and built a **Memorial Cottage** on the original Smith cabin site. According to Junius Wells, the 27- x 54-inch gray **log cabin hearthstone** was placed in the **Memorial Cottage** in the same location as it was when in the **log cabin.** The hearthstone was the central item of importance, with the Memorial Cottage built around it. He said, "This hearthstone shall be the altar on which this home shall rest" (ERA Feb. 1906, p. 318). The Memorial Cottage served as a visitors center from 1905 to 1959, when it was torn down. In 1961 it was replaced by two buildings: a **visitors center** and a **director's building,** separated by a reflecting pond. The pond was later removed. In 1961 the **hearthstone** was moved to the newer visitors center, 200′ SE of the original position. The "new" visitors center is staffed by missionaries.

**2. LOG CABIN SITE.** The log cabin site is located 200′ NW of the visitors center, and behind the director's building. It is identified by a **small stone marker.** This was the site of the original **log cabin** in which the Prophet Joseph Smith was born on that wintery day of December 23, 1805.

According to old surveys, the log cabin either straddled or was near the

*Log Cabin Site, Sharon, VT, where the Prophet Joseph Smith was born. (Photo by George E. Anderson, 1907; courtesy of LDSCA)*

Royalton-Sharon township line. Although the township line varied with different surveys, Joseph Smith in his history indicates he was born in "the town [township] of Sharon, Windsor County, State of Vermont" (JS-H 1:3). A newspaper article written in 1947 by Judge A. G. Whiting, who in the early 1900s was a law graduate in the office of Tarbell and Whitham, and who assisted Junius Wells to "clear titles and arrange for details" pertaining to the site of the Joseph Smith Memorial Monument, explains: "When Joseph Smith was born, the farmhouse was located in Sharon, but it was later discovered that the boundary between Royalton and Sharon had been changed more than once by various surveys made at intervals. The town line as finally established runs outside the foundations of the old house, close to the old cellar wall, which remained standing. The site of the monument was determined to be just over the town line in Sharon" (ERA Jan. 1947, p. 18). The cellar wall and portions of the foundation were still visible at the time the farm was purchased in 1905.

The **front doorstep** of the original log cabin is located near the small stone marker. The plaque on the doorstep reads:

> THIS STONE WAS THE FRONT DOORSTEP OF THE
> SOLOMON MACK HOME WHERE JOSEPH SMITH WAS BORN.
> IT WAS ALSO THE BACK DOORSTEP OF THE COTTAGE
> WHICH STOOD HERE FROM 1905 UNTIL 1959.

The **old well** that supplied water for the Smiths is located a short distance west of the director's home.

**3. JOSEPH SMITH MONUMENT.** Near the spot where the Prophet was born in Sharon Township, a granite shaft, or obclisk, 38½ feet high was erected as a **monument to the Prophet Joseph Smith.** Each foot of the dark Barre granite shaft represents a year of the Prophet's life. It weighs 39 tons and is made of one single piece of rock. It is 4′ square at the bottom and 3′ square at the top. The monument consists of five sections—two bases, an inscription stone, an ornate cap, and the shaft. Including its base, the monument stands 50 feet tall and weighs over 100 tons. Its pieces were hauled first by train, and then by horse-drawn wagons from

*Joseph Smith Monument, Sharon, VT. (1972)*

the Marr and Gordon quarry in Barre—about 35 miles away (ERA Jan. 1947, p. 18). **Transportation obstacles** included weak bridges, muddy roads, and Dairy Hill. With 20 horses pulling a great wagon with wheels 20 inches wide, with the use of pulleys, and with frozen ground that was an answer to prayer, the task was accomplished. Nearly seven weeks passed before all the granite pieces were on the hilltop. It took 13 days to take the shaft 2½

*Joseph Smith Monument Base Stones, which weigh 18 tons, Sharon, VT. (Courtesy of LDSCA; 1905)*

*Joseph Smith Monument Shaft, Sharon, VT, is 38 ½ feet high and weighs 39 tons. (Courtesy of LDSCA; 1907)*

miles up Dairy Hill Road, and the monument was completed only 4 days before the dedication services. Junius F. Wells felt that it was divine intervention when the muddy road froze and the heavy shaft could be transported.

Both the memorial cottage and the monument were **dedicated on Dec. 23, 1905**—the 100th anniversary of the Prophet's birth—by **President Joseph F. Smith,** nephew of the Prophet. In the dedicatory prayer President Smith said:

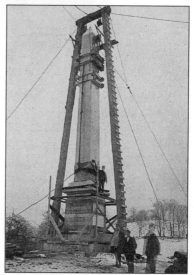

*Joseph Smith Monument Stone Setting, Sharon, VT. (Photo by Junius F. Wells, 1905; courtesy of LDSCA)*

We dedicate to thee the ground on which stands this monument, that it may be sacred and most holy. We dedicate the foundation, typical of the foundation thou hast laid, of apostles and prophets, with Jesus Christ, thy son, as the chief corner stone. We dedicate the base, as typifying the rock of revelation on which thy Church is built. We dedicate the die, with its inscriptions, as appropriate to the whole design. We dedicate the capstone as a sign of the glorious crown that thy servant Joseph has secured unto himself through his integrity to thy cause, and of that similar reward which shall grace the head of each of his faithful followers. We dedicate the spire, as a token of the inspired man of God whom thou didst make indeed a polished shaft in thine hand, reflecting the light of heaven, even thy glorious light, unto the children of men (ERA Feb. 1906, pp. 324–25).

After the dedicatory prayer the monument was unveiled and tears of joy filled the eyes of those present.

*Joseph Smith Monument Dedication, 23 December 1905, Sharon, VT. (Courtesy of LDSCA)*

*President Joseph F. Smith (Ca. 1905)*

On the day of the dedication, Elder Francis M. Lyman told those present, "You will find that travel will increase on this road, and that it [the monument] will become one of the most famous spots in Vermont, or any section of the United States" (CoCo 3A).

Two sides of the base bear inscriptions. One side reads: "Sacred to the memory of Joseph Smith, the Prophet. Born here 23d December, 1805; martyred, Carthage, Illinois, 27th June, 1844." On another side is the quotation of James 1:5 (the New Testament scripture which led the boy Joseph to pray for guidance in the spring of 1820), and a brief history of the Prophet's life and accomplishments (MTVU 12–13).

Over 30,000 people from all over the world visit this monument every year (CoCo 3A, 15A). To Latter-day Saints this site is sacred. Here is the beginning! This was the birthplace of the prophet of God through whom the fulness of the gospel of Jesus Christ was restored to the earth. And as light is reflected from the pyramid-shaped top of the obelisk, visitors are reminded that the light of heaven is reflected to the children of men through prophets of God, and that salvation comes through the Savior, Jesus Christ.

### ■ The Old Turnpike Road, Rock Walls, Solomon Mack "Traditional" Home Site, and Patriarch Hill

Behind the granite Joseph Smith Memorial is a small dirt road leading downhill to the Old Turnpike Road (see map). The Turnpike is about ½ mile from the monument and the top of Patriarch Hill is about 1 ¼ miles from the monument. Automobiles may be driven to the "traditional" Daniel Mack cabin foundation, and 4x4 vehicles may be driven to the top of Patriarch Hill.

**4. OLD TURNPIKE ROAD AND ROCK WALLS.** The old Turnpike Road stretched from Boston to Montreal and was used by the Macks and Smiths as they traveled to and from Sharon Village. By the road is a marker that reads:

THE OLD TURNPIKE ROAD

THE TURNPIKE WHICH WAS THE MAIN HIGHWAY THROUGH THIS PART OF THE COUNTRY WHEN THE MACKS LIVED HERE PASSED BY THE MACK HOME AT THIS SPOT ACROSS THE STREAM FROM THE FRONT YARD OF THE MACK RESIDENCE. REMNANTS OF THE OLD [ROCK] WALLS THAT WERE BUILT ON EACH SIDE OF THE HIGHWAY CAN STILL BE SEEN IN PLACES.

**5. SOLOMON MACK'S TRADITIONAL HOME SITE.** Solomon Mack's "traditional" home site with its large foundation and cellar wall stones can be seen on the east side of the Old Turnpike immediately east of the stream bed. **Solomon** and his wife, **Lydia Gates,** were the parents of **Lucy Mack Smith,** which made them **Joseph Smith's** grandparents. This site has a marker that reads:

*Traditional Home Site of Solomon and Lydia Mack,
Sharon, VT. View to the west. (Photo by George E.
Anderson, 1907; courtesy of LDSCA)*

### SOLOMON MACK HOME

THE SOLOMON MACK FARM, 100 ACRES, WAS PURCHASED BY HIM IN
1804. AN EXTRA HOUSE ON IT WAS RENTED TO HIS SON-IN-LAW,
JOSEPH SMITH, SR. THIS OLD CELLAR IS ALL THAT REMAINS OF THE
SOLOMON MACK HOME. NEARBY MAY BE SEEN FOUNDATIONS FOR THE
OUT BUILDINGS.

**6. OLD STONE BRIDGE.** The Old Stone Bridge is located upstream
(north) of the Solomon Mack home site about ¼ mile on the west
side of the Turnpike. A marker at the bridge reads:

### THE OLD STONE BRIDGE

THIS BRIDGE IS TYPICAL OF THE EARLY SMALL BRIDGES IN NEW ENG-
LAND. IT IS MADE ENTIRELY OF STONES AND WAS HERE BEFORE 1804,
WHEN THE SOLOMON MACK FAMILY PURCHASED THE FARM. THE OLD
TURNPIKE WHICH WAS THE MAIN HIGHWAY THROUGH THE COUNTRY
CROSSED THIS BRIDGE AT THAT TIME.

**7. DANIEL G. MACK "TRADITIONAL" HOME SITE.** On the west side of
the turnpike about ¼ mile north of the Old Bridge, is the "traditional" **Daniel G. Mack Home Site** and foundations. Daniel was a
brother of Lucy Mack Smith.

A marker at the site reads:

### The Daniel G. Mack Home

This old cellar and foundation marks the spot where the Daniel Mack family probably lived for many years after the Solomon Mack farm was sold by Daniel's father in 1811. Lydia Gates Mack, the mother of Daniel and Lucy Mack Smith, lived with Daniel until her death about 1817.

Lucy Mack indicated her mother's death resulted from injuries sustained in a wagon accident. Lydia Mack died two years after Lucy left to go to Palmyra, NY. This suggests that Lydia died in 1818 (HJS 61–62). Though Lucy Mack indicates her mother died while living with her son in Royalton, the question remains, where in Royalton Township? Lydia's burial site has not been located.

**8. Patriarch Hill.** A trail to the top of Patriarch Hill goes east from the Old Turnpike Road at a point north of the Old Stone Bridge and just north of the visitor restrooms, or immediately north of a road that leads up to the Joseph Smith Memorial Monument. The hike from the Old Turnpike and back to the Turnpike is about 1¼ miles up and down a rather steep hill, 500′ in elevation above the stream where the trail starts. A road for tractors or 4x4 vehicles also goes to the top from the Old Turnpike Road. It is also possible to drive a vehicle to the top from the Village of Sharon.

Patriarch Hill provides a beautiful **panoramic view** of the Solomon Mack Farm and Joseph Smith Memorial. The view is worth the hike. A **marker** on the top of the hill identifies the point where four townships meet: Sharon, Royalton, Tunbridge, and Strafford (see map).

**9. Camp Joseph.** June 27, 1998, on the anniversary of the Prophet Joseph Smith's martyrdom, Elder Marlin K. Jensen of the Seventy, president of the North America Northeast Area, dedicated a new camping facility at the site of the Prophet's birthplace. The camp, named Camp Joseph, includes "a 40-by-50-foot log lodge, covered pavilion, 15 log cabins, restroom facilities, an athletic field, an archery range and a pond for swimming." Camp Joseph makes it possible for "individuals, families and Church groups to stay on the site where Joseph Smith was born Dec. 23, 1805" (CN Jul. 25, 1998, p. 7).

# ■ Royalton Township

The **Township of Royalton** is located between Sharon Township on the east and Bethel Township on the west. Only three small villages are or have been located in the Township of Royalton: South Royalton, Royalton, and North Royalton. All three are near the White River on State 14.

A part of **Solomon Mack's 100-acre farm** was in Royalton Township, although he lived in Sharon Township. The cabin Joseph Smith Sr. rented from Solomon Mack was built close to the line between the townships of Royalton and Sharon.

**Joseph Smith Sr.** and his wife, **Lucy,** lived in Royalton Township twice: (1) Once in 1803–4 for a few months after they sold their farm in Tunbridge and before they settled in what was then

*William Smith*

Sharon Township in the cabin owned by Lucy's father, Solomon, where Joseph Smith Jr. was born, and (2) after Joseph Smith's birth in what was then Sharon township, Joseph Sr. and Lucy moved back to Tunbridge, then after a short time moved back to Royalton Township (about 1809–11).

**Ephraim,** son of Joseph Sr. and Lucy Mack Smith, was born here on Mar. 13, 1810, and died 11 days later on Mar. 24. Their next son, **William,** was also born in Royalton Township on Mar. 13, 1811, just before the Joseph Smith Sr. family moved to West Lebanon, NH (HJS 46; ReS 61).

In 1816 **Daniel Mack's** home "in Royalton" provided shelter and care for Daniel Mack's mother, **Lydia Gates Mack,** (Joseph Smith Jr.'s grandmother). Lydia had been hurt in a wagon accident between Norwich and Royalton as she was traveling with her daughter Lucy and grandchildren, including Joseph, as they started their journey toward Palmyra, NY, in 1816. Lydia remained with her son Daniel until she died two years later (HJS 61–62). As Lucy Mack wrote about the Macks living in Royalton, she did not use the words township or village, so it is difficult to determine where Daniel or other Macks lived in Royalton Township.

**Elias Smith,** remembered as one of the best representatives of

*Albert Carrington*

Mormon jurisprudence in the history of Utah, was born in Royalton Township on Sept. 6, 1804 (BiE 1:719). In addition, **Charles Durkee,** the sixth governor of Utah, was born here in 1802 (HOU 655–60). Durkee eventually emigrated to Wisconsin and served in Congress. Later he served as Utah's governor from 1865 until 1869 (MoS 153–54). **Albert Carrington,** an Apostle from 1870 to 1885, was born here on Jan. 8, 1813 (CHFT 619).

## ■ SOUTH ROYALTON

South Royalton is the largest of the three villages in Royalton Township. It is located on State 14, five miles NW of the village of Sharon. It is on the south side of White River, ½ mile south of the junction of State 14 and 110.

*South Royalton, VT; looking NW.*
*(Ca. 1900; courtesy of LDSCA)*

At South Royalton, on the evenings of Dec. 22–23, 1905, in a hall over **Woodard's Hotel, President Joseph F. Smith** presided at meetings held in conjunction with the dedication of the **Joseph Smith Monument and Memorial Cottage** (PaD).

## ■ ROYALTON—Burial Place of Stephen and Sarah Smith

The small village of Royalton is located two miles west of South Royalton on State 14, or seven miles NW of the village of Sharon on the north side of the White River.

Joseph Smith Sr.'s brother and sister **Stephen** and **Sarah Smith** are buried side-by-side in the Royalton cemetery in the

*Tombstone of Stephen Smith, Royalton, VT.*
*(Photo by George E. Anderson, 1907; courtesy of LDSCA)*

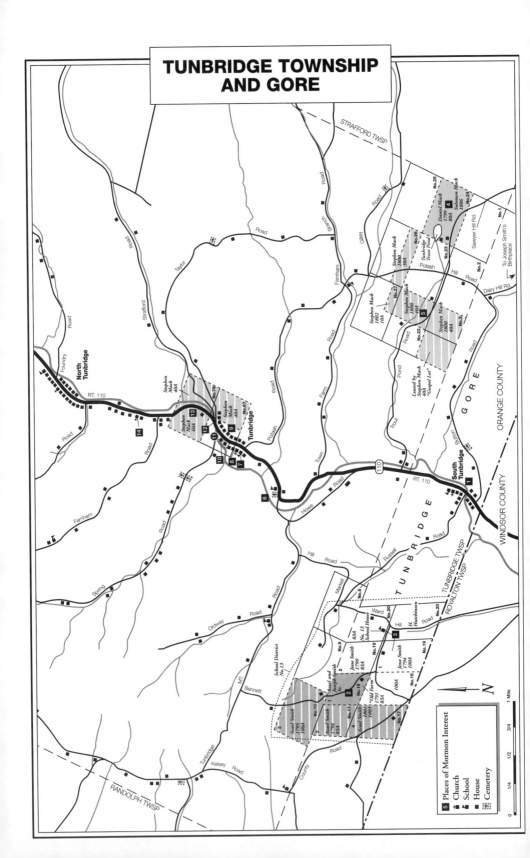

# TUNBRIDGE TOWNSHIP AND GORE

fourth row of graves in the center of the cemetery, about 25 feet from the road (State 14). Stephen's black tombstone reads: "In memory of Stephen son of Asael and Mary Smith—Died July 25, 1802 Age 17" (HC 2:443). Sarah, the youngest daughter, married Joseph Stafford in 1809 and remained in Vermont until her death May 27, 1824. There is another child, perhaps a cousin, buried close to Stephen.

In 1780 Royalton was the scene of the most frightful Indian raid ever made on Vermont settlers. A monument marks this event. This village is also the birthplace of Frederick Billings, founder of the University of California.

## ■ Tunbridge Township[2]

Home of the Smiths and Macks for 25 years, and birthplace of Alvin, Hyrum, Sophronia, and Samuel Smith, the township of Tunbridge is located immediately north of Royalton Township and NNW of Sharon Township, about 20 miles NW of White River Junction. It was settled after the Revolutionary War, mostly along what is now State 110, which follows the First Branch of the White River going basically north and south through the middle of the township (see map).

Like Royalton Township, Tunbridge Township is sparsely settled, having just three villages: South Tunbridge, Tunbridge, and North Tunbridge. It is important to Mormon history because the Prophet Joseph Smith's ancestors on both the Mack and Smith lines lived here for about 25 years (Smiths 1791–ca. 1816 and Macks 1795–ca. 1820). Joseph's grandfather Asael Smith moved to Tunbridge Township in 1791, and his grandfather Solomon Mack moved here in 1799. Tunbridge was officially organized as a town on Mar. 21, 1786. It was probably named after Benning Wentworth's friend, Viscount Tunbridge.

**1. SOUTH TUNBRIDGE IN TUNBRIDGE GORE.** South Tunbridge is located in Orange County on State 110 about 3 miles north of South Royalton Village and ¼ mile north of the Orange–Windsor line. It is in the center of South Tunbridge that Russel Road turns NW toward the **Asael Smith Farm.** After crossing over a bridge on

---

[2] Dr. LaMar E. Garrard did the research necessary to identify property rented or purchased by the Smith and Mack families in Tunbridge Township.

State 110, the dirt road
goes west to the farm.

A strip of unsurveyed
land ³⁄₄ mile wide
stretched along the SW
border of Tunbridge
Township between the
boundaries of Tunbridge
and Royalton Township
before 1785. This strip of
land resulted from a sur-
veying error and legally
belonged to neither town.
Such mistakes were not

*Tunbridge Gore, Orange Co., VT. Location of
Smith families' farms. Looking east. (Photo by
George E. Anderson, 1907; courtesy of LDSCA)*

uncommon and shrewd individuals were on the lookout for these
areas, which were called "gores." In 1785 this particular gore became
a part of Tunbridge Township and was known as **Tunbridge Gore.**
South Tunbridge is the village in the gore (OBT), and the farms of
**Asael, Jesse,** and **Joseph Jr.** were all in Tunbridge Gore.

**2. ASAEL AND JOSEPH SMITH'S "OLD FARM" AND ASAEL'S OTHER
FARMS.** Asael and Joseph Smith's "old farm" of 83 acres is located
three miles NW of South Tunbridge. To get to the farm, go NW
out of South Tunbridge on Russell Road ("Gore Road") up Rus-

*Joseph Smith Sr. Farm, Tunbridge
Gore, VT. Looking east—auto and
figures are by the home site. (1972)*

sell Brook 1³⁄₄ miles. Turn left
(south) onto Ward Hill Road for
.6 mile, then right .4 mile (past
the Ward Hill School) to a fork
in the road, then to the right on
Bennett Road for .3 mile to the
center of Asael's 83-acre farm
and a **foundation** of a building
that is about 20 feet west of the
road. According to tradition, this
is the foundation of Asael Smith's
cabin where, later, Joseph Smith
Sr. lived, and where his children
Alvin, Hyrum, Sophronia, and
Samuel were born. Bennett Road
goes through the middle of two
of Asael's farms (see map).

Asael Smith (1744–1830) was Joseph Smith's grandfather. He married **Mary Duty** in 1767 and lived in New Hampshire and Massachusetts before moving to Tunbridge Gore in 1791. After four generations of Smiths had lived in Topsfield, MA, it was Asael who made the move to another state, Vermont.

*Foundation of Joseph Smith Sr. home in Tunbridge Gore, VT. Looking west. (1972)*

In the spring of 1791, **Asael Smith** and his oldest son, Jesse, left Ipswich, MA, to look for a new home in Vermont. They soon returned with the news that they had purchased an 83-acre farm in Tunbridge, VT, at a cost of £26, about a dollar an acre. The acreage they purchased was in the "gore," WNW of South Tunbridge. The deed to the farm was dated June 21, 1791. The farm was identified as Lot No. 18 North (TTR 1:324; 3:446) (see map). The farm was in school district 13, and Asael's son, Jesse, was appointed later as a District No. 13 Trustee.

The two older boys, **Jesse** (23) and **Joseph Sr.** (20) went to the "gore" ahead of the family. They cleared off **land** and built a small rough **log cabin.** "It was loosely built after the mode of building log huts, say 14 by 10 feet. The covering was the bark of the elm, . . ." remembered young John Smith, who was age 10 when the move came (RoJS; JSN 101). In Oct. 1791, Asael (age 46), his wife Mary, and their 11 children left Ipswich and settled in the small log cabin in Tunbridge Gore. Their children were Jesse (b. 1768), Priscilla (b. 1769), Joseph (b. 1771—father of the Prophet Joseph Smith), Asael Jr. (b. 1773), Mary (b. 1775), Samuel (b. 1777), Silas (b. 1779), John (b. 1781), Susannah (b. 1783), Stephen (b. 1785, d. 1802—buried in Royalton), and Sarah (b. 1789, md. Joseph Sanford 1809, d. 1824—buried in Royalton near Stephen's grave).

Father **Asael** worked as a cooper and a farmer in Tunbridge, and eventually purchased more **land,** including three contiguous farms. The three farms included Lot 17 North, 83 acres, Nov. 27, 1794, for £12 (TTR 2:101, 121); Lot 10, 100 acres, Dec. 23, 1795 for £60 (TTR 2:211), Lot 17, 100 acres, Sept. 5, 1801, with Silas for $545. Asael's four farms totaled 366 acres (TTR 3:75, 302, 345) (see map).

B. H. Roberts wrote that Asael was "a man of noble independence of mind, yet of child-like humility" (CHC 1:12). Asael's letter to Jacob Town dated Jan. 14, 1796, indicated he believed America was the promised land, and that the stone is now cut out, as spoken by the prophet Daniel. In 1799 he wrote an "Address to His Family" as a sort of "last words" to them, yet he lived for another 30 years. He encouraged his children to trust in God and to believe in immortality. He affirmed that religion was necessary, that God is no respecter of persons, that marriage is predestined, that children should help one another, that the Constitution of the United States was of God, and that Christ had the most important role in men's salvation (CHC 1:9–12).

It was Asael who prophesied of his grandson Joseph Smith's destiny. Asael said, "It has been borne in upon my soul that one of my descendants will promulgate a work to revolutionize the world of religious faith" (ECH 25). Of this prophecy, Joseph Smith later said, "My grandfather, Asael Smith, long ago predicted that there would be a prophet raised up in his family, and my grandmother [Mary] was fully satisfied that it was fulfilled in me" (HC 2:443). "Asael, Mary, and eight of their children were still alive when the Book of Mormon was first brought to their areas. Only Jesse and two sisters [Mary and Susan] failed to believe" (JSN 111, 211–12). The four sons who believed were Joseph Smith Sr., Asael Jr., Silas, and John. Two sons served prominently in the Church: Joseph Smith Sr. was Church Patriarch for seven years (1833–40), and an assistant counselor to the First Presidency for three years (1837–40); John also served as assistant counselor to the First Presidency (1837–44), Church Patriarch (1849–54), and was president of three stakes: one at Adam-ondi-Ahman, one in the Nauvoo area, and one in Salt Lake City. John was the father of George A. Smith, counselor to Brigham Young (JSN 111, 143–44, 217–18).

Asael lived in Tunbridge Gore for about 20–25 years, then, like his son Silas, who had moved earlier (ca. 1806–09), Asael moved to Stockholm, St. Lawrence Co., NY. In 1830 his son Joseph and grandson Don Carlos visited Asael in Silas's home at Stockholm and presented him with a copy of the Book of Mormon, just off the press. Asael accepted it as true, but was too weak to be baptized at that time and died Oct. 30, 1830, at age 86, shortly after his son's visit.

Asael's wife, **Mary,** was 93 years old when in 1836 she traveled to Kirtland to visit her relatives. The Prophet Joseph and Hyrum met her at Fairport Harbor and transported her to Kirtland (HC 2:442). Mary intended to have Joseph the Prophet baptize her, but died soon after her arrival in Kirtland (JSN 111–16). She is buried in the cemetery by the Kirtland Temple.

**The old farm** (Lot No. 18 North) became **Joseph Smith Sr.'s farm.** In a letter to Jacob P. Town dated Jan. 14, 1796, Asael said he expected to move into a new house the next spring and "begin again on an entire new farm" (HC 1:286–87; CHC 1:7–8; JSN 108–23). He said his son **Joseph** was to "be married in a few days" (Joseph was married to Lucy Mack on Jan. 24, 1796 by Hezekiah Hutchinson, town clerk), and that his son would "live on the **old farm** [of 1791—Lot No. 18 North] and carry it on at the halves, which half I hope will nearly furnish my family with food whilst I with my four youngest sons shall endeavor to bring to another farm etc." (JSN 118). Lucy Mack Smith said they owned a "handsome farm" in Tunbridge where they farmed for six years (HJS 32).

*Hyrum Smith*

The "old farm" in the "gore" was the **birthplace** of at least four of the first six children of Lucy and Joseph Sr.: a **son** who died at childbirth; **Alvin** (b. Feb. 11, 1798, d. Nov. 19, 1823 in Palmyra [JSH 1:4; D&C 137, 138]); **Hyrum** (b. Feb. 9, 1800, d. June 27, 1844), **Sophronia** (b. May 16, 1803); and **Samuel Harrison** (b. March 13, 1808, d. July 30, 1844). It is very possible that the **foundation** by the road and near the middle of the farm was a part of the home where these children were born.

After living on the "old farm" for six years, Joseph and Lucy rented out the "old farm" and moved in 1802 to **Randolph Township,** where they ran a store. After losing money in a ginseng venture, they moved back to the "old farm" that same year, 1802. Sophronia was born May 16, 1803. The farm was sold for $800, half its assessed value. In addition, Lucy used her $1000 wedding present from John Mudget and Stephen Mack to clear up all their debts, and the family moved to **Royalton** for a few months, then to **Sharon,** where the future prophet Joseph was born (HJS 31–32, 37, 40, 46).

The third and last time the Joseph Smith Sr. family lived in Tunbridge Township was in 1807–8 after moving from Sharon. **Samuel Harrison** was born here on Mar. 13, 1808.

**3. JESSE SMITH FARMS AND DISTRICT NO. 13 SCHOOLHOUSE (WARD SCHOOL). Jesse Smith,** Asael's oldest son and Joseph Smith Sr.'s brother, married Hannah Peabody on Jan. 20, 1792, and later purchased two **farms** located east and southeast of and adjoining the "old farm" of his father Asael and his brother Joseph Smith Sr. Jesse bought a 100-acre farm (Lot 19 South) on Nov. 19, 1794 (TTR 2:101, 168, 378, 447), and then on Feb. 5, 1799, he purchased an additional 83-acre farm (Lot 19 North) (TTR 2:380, 464; 3:138). The road to the "old farm" goes through the middle of Jesse's two farms (see map). He also owned other properties in Tunbridge and purchased Lots 10 and 17 North from his father, Asael, in 1805.

The **District No. 13 schoolhouse (Ward School)** is located ³⁄₄ mile east of the Asael/Joseph Smith Sr. log cabin site and ¼ mile east of the center of Jesse's farm. It is about 100 yards west of Hill Road at the corner where a right turn is made off Hill Road to go to the Asael Smith Farm (see map).

*District No. 13 Schoolhouse, Tunbridge Gore, VT, where the Smith children attended school, and perhaps where Joseph Smith Sr. taught. (Photo by George E. Anderson, 1907; courtesy of LDSCA)*

**Jesse Smith,** who lived near the schoolhouse, was the Trustee of School District No. 13, so his children would have attended this school. There is also the possibility that **Alvin** and **Hyrum,** Joseph Smith Sr.'s children, attended school here in 1807–8. There is also a tradition that **Joseph Smith Sr.** taught school here.

The schoolhouse, with some remodeling, still stands and is used as a hunting lodge.

**4. SOLOMON AND DANIEL MACK FARM IN SE TUNBRIDGE TOWNSHIP. Solomon Mack,** Joseph Smith's grandfather on his mother's side of the family, moved from Gilsum, NH, to Tunbridge Township about 1799, then in 1804 moved onto his newly acquired 100-acre farm in Sharon, birthplace of the Prophet Joseph Smith. Apparently Solomon moved back to Tunbridge in 1804 when Joseph Smith Sr. rented Solomon's log cabin and farm in Sharon. Then, when Joseph Sr. moved from Solomon's Sharon farm in 1807, Solomon returned to the farm and lived there until he sold it in 1811. He then lived in Tunbridge again until he moved to Gilsum, NH, in 1818, where he died on Aug. 23, 1820, at age 88. His tombstone says age 84, which is evidently an error (JSN 25). Solomon lived in Tunbridge three times: 1799–1804, 1805–7, and 1811–18. He probably lived with either of his two sons, Stephen or Daniel, until he purchased 100 acres from Daniel in 1806.

In the SE corner of Tunbridge Township were properties of **Solomon Mack** and his two sons, **Daniel** and **Stephen** (HJS 21–28). One-half mile north of the church in South Tunbridge is Trout Pond Road, which goes east from State 110 to the Mack Farms. From State 110 it is 1.6 miles to the center of Stephen's farms and 2½ miles to the center of Daniel and Solomon's farm (see map).

**Daniel** purchased Lot No. 24 (80 acres) on June 17, 1799, in Tunbridge Township, just north of the "gore" and joining the Strafford Township line. **Solomon Mack** purchased this land from Daniel on May 3, 1806, for $200, along with two mortgages for $110 and $343, which Solomon assumed. The deed was witnessed by Joseph Smith Sr. and Hezekiah Hutchinson, a local justice of the peace (TTR 3:380). Although it is unknown where Solomon lived in Tunbridge from 1799 to 1804, it can be assumed he lived on Lot 24 for ten years: 1805–7 and 1811–18. Whether he lived with his son Daniel or in his own cabin on his own 100 acres of property is unknown. Lucy said her mother, Lydia, lived with Daniel in Royalton for the last two years of her life (1816–18; HJS 61), so questions remain concerning the location of Daniel's, Solomon's, and Lydia's home during 1816–18.

**5. STEPHEN MACK FARMS.** One-half mile separates the Stephen and Solomon Mack Farms. Stephen's is ½ mile west of Solomon's, with Trout Pond Road going through the center of Stephen's farm. Stephen Mack purchased the following land in 1800 as a part of an $8000 purchase from John Mudget: East half of Lot No. 3 (40 acres); East half of Lot No. 22 (40 acres); 30 acres of Lot No. 26; 10 acres of Lot No. 27; and 6 acres of Lot No. 23 (see map). He also leased the west half of Lot No. 3 which was a "Gospel Lot." In Tunbridge Township they also had "minister lots," "school lots," and "mill lots" (TTR 2:122, 558).

**Stephen** was a prominent and prosperous farmer and businessman in Tunbridge Township. He was born in 1766 as the second child of Solomon and Lydia Mack. His intimate friend and neighbor (see map), Horace Stanley, called Stephen "Major Mack," and said that Stephen was a man of great enterprise and energy. He owned a saw mill, an oil mill, fulling mill (cleans and presses cloth), a clothier's shop, tainter bars, and a shop for cutting and heading rails. He also conducted a mercantile and tinning business in Chelsea, the Orange Co. seat.

In the early 1800s Stephen moved to Pontiac, MI, where he operated stores, a saw mill, and a flour mill. He made the turnpike road from Detroit to Pontiac at his own expense (Horace Stanley's statement in HJS 22–23). Stephen is buried in the Oak Hill Cemetery at Pontiac, MI.

Note the Potash Mill Road and Dairy Hill Road that run between the Mack farms (see map). Dairy Hill Road goes south to the Joseph Smith Memorial.

**6. JOHN MUDGET GRAVE.** At a point 1 ¾ miles north of the South Tunbridge Church, just past a bend in the road, is a cemetery where **John Mudget,** business partner of Stephen Mack, is buried. His small gray slate tombstone, located in the SE corner of the cemetery, reads: "In memory of John Mudget who died January 27, 1801 Age 29."

When John Mudget conversed with his friend and business partner Stephen Mack about Lucy Mack's wedding gift, Mudget said, "Lucy ought to have something worth naming, and I will give her just as much as you will." When Stephen offered Lucy $500 John Mudget matched it, making $1000 as a wedding gift for Lucy (HJS 32).

## ■ *Tunbridge*

Tunbridge, also called Tunbridge Center, is 6 miles north of South Royalton on State 110, and 2.7 miles north of South Tunbridge.

**7. TUNBRIDGE TOWN CLERK AND LIBRARY BUILDING.** The Tunbridge Town Clerk and Library Building is located on the south end of the "business district" of Tunbridge on the west side of State 110. The **marriage record** of **Joseph Smith Sr.** and **Lucy Mack** is located here, along with land records (deeds, etc.).

In 1793 **Asael** was chosen as one of three Selectmen who managed Tunbridge's town affairs. He occasionally served as modera-

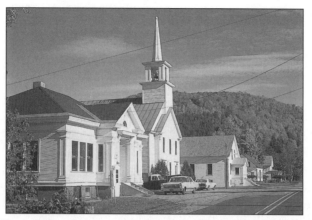

*Town Hall and Congregational Church, Tunbridge, VT. (1972)*

tor and highway surveyor. Asael's son **Jesse** served as a Selectman and Town Clerk also.

Before **Asael** moved to Tunbridge, he expressed his humor by listing his taxable property in a **poem.** It was later recovered among the "scraps on file" in the town archives of Topsfield, MA:

> *To the Selectmen of Topsfield*
>
> I have two polls, the one is poor,
> I have three cows and want five more,
> I have no horse, but fifteen sheep—
> No more than these this year I keep;
> Steers that's two years old, one pair,
> Two calves I have, all over hair,
> Three heifers two years old I own,
> One heifer calf that's poorly grown.
> My land is acres eighty-two,
> Which search the records, you'll find true.
> And this is all I have in store—
> I'll thank you if you'll tax no more.
> Asael Smith (JSN 98–99)

**8. CONGREGATIONAL MEETINGHOUSE.** Just north of the Town Clerk and Library Building is the Tunbridge Meetinghouse, built in 1838. This is not the building or the site of the Congregational Church with which Asael Smith and his family would have been associated (see # 14, "The Congregational Church").

**9. VILLAGE STORE.** In the middle of Tunbridge on the east side of State 110 is the village store, where tradition indicates that Joseph met his future wife, Lucy Mack, who was working in this store for her brother, Stephen Mack (HJS 31–32). Horace Stanley, Stephen's neighbor, reported that Stephen ran a store in Tunbridge that

*Village Store, Tunbridge, VT, where, according to tradition, Joseph Smith Sr. met Lucy Mack. (Courtesy of Charlotte Barry; 1917)*

was two miles away from Stanley's home. Stanley also reported that Stephen conducted a mercantile and tinning business in Chelsea, 6 miles north of Tunbridge Village (HJS 22).

**10. SAWMILL AND BUSINESS BUILDINGS OF STEPHEN MACK.** A half block NW of the village store and between State 110 and the stream—

*Stephen Mack Sawmill, Tunbridge Village, VT. (1972)*

First Branch of the White River—are several business buildings that were leased, then owned by Stephen Mack. These buildings are on both sides of Spring Road that goes west through the **Mill Bridge** (covered). The **blacksmith shop** near the bridge, along with other buildings, has been converted to other uses.

Stephen leased the land from Elias Curtis Apr. 6, 1803, for $40

> for the purpose of erecting an oil mill, fulling mill [cleans and presses cloth], clothers shop and tainter bars [for dyeing] and also a shop for cutting and heading rails with two homes all on a flat of ground west of Samuel Bement's shop in Tunbridge aforesaid betwixt the road and branch also for a carding mashein [machine] in the upper part of the oil mill to be erected and set to work the present year with the loading

mashein [sic] the fulling mill and nailing works to be erected in one year and six months from this date. . . . yielding and paying one ear of corn annually if demanded on the first day of December and paying all lawful assessments and taxes" (Indenture of Lease dated April 6, 1803, TTR 3:62–63).

On May 17, 1803, Stephen Mack leased the **sawmill** that had been built by Elias Curtis (TTR 3:60–61), and by 1808 Stephen owned the **sawmill** and the **carding machine.** The red brick and lumber building that houses the sawmill is located near the SE corner of State 110 and Spring Road, near the covered bridge. Stephen's sawmill and Curtis's gristmill were water powered, supplied by a pond behind a dam just north of the covered bridge.

**11. MILL BRIDGE (COVERED) 1883.** A picturesque covered bridge dated 1883 crosses over the First Branch of the White River near the Stephen Mack sawmill. Spring Road passes over the bridge.

**12. CURTIS AND BEMENT DAM.** The dam located on the stream just north of the sawmill was built by Elias Curtis and Samuel Bement who operated a **gristmill** with the water from the pond created by the dam. Stephen Mack used water from the same pond to run his **sawmill** and other businesses (TTR 3:62–63). The **dam,** built before 1803, can be seen upstream from the covered bridge.

**13. STEPHEN MACK LAND IN/NEAR TUNBRIDGE.** Besides the sawmill and business lots near the Mill Bridge, Stephen owned 120 acres on the NE end of **Tunbridge Village:** Lot No. 78 (80 acres) purchased from John Mudget, and the east half of Lot No. 67 (40 acres) (TTR 2:122, 384, 552) (see map).

**14. THE CONGREGATIONAL CHURCH AND THE UNIVERSALIST SOCIETY MEETING PLACE SITE.** On the west side of State 110 at a point 1.1 miles north of the Tunbridge Town Clerk and Library Building is the site of the Congregational Church in Tunbridge. "According to Rev. James Ramage, the church 'was used for secular as well as sacred purposes, all town meetings being held there. Different denominations held services in it from time to time'" (Lamar Garrard, "The Smith Family and the First Congregational Church in Tunbridge"; A key resource for that paper was a publication by a Rev. James Ramage entitled "Church Edifices," in Centennial Celebration of the Congregational Church, Tunbridge, Vermont [Montpelier, Vt.: Watchman Publishing Co., 1892]). One of those "different denominations" was the Universalist Society organized in 1797 by Asael Smith and 15 others, including his sons Jesse and Joseph Smith Sr. This group objected to paying taxes for the erection of a church building designated for a particular denomination, but agreed to help financially by buying pews, giving them the right to use the building. "A Universalist Society was formed in Tunbridge, Vermont, and its members filed formal notice of exemption from 'any tax towards the support of any teacher of any different denomination whatever,' a reference to the normal town tax for Congregational worship. The moderator of this meeting was Asael Smith, and three of the sixteen signers were Asael Smith, together with Jesse Smith and Joseph Smith, his oldest sons" (JSN 106). **Asael Smith** had also been a pew holder in the Congregational Church at Topsfield, MA, but he advocated the basic beliefs of John Murray and the believing Christian Universalists. According to the 1803 New Hampshire Convention, Universalist beliefs were summarized: "We believe there is one God, whose nature is love, revealed in one Lord Jesus Christ, by one Holy Spirit of grace, who will finally restore the whole family of mankind to holiness and happiness" (JSN 105).

The original Congregational Church building no longer stands, but the site is noted on USGS maps of 1924 and 1944.

# ■ Randolph Township

## ■ RANDOLPH CENTER

Randolph is located 15 miles NW of South Royalton on State 12. Interstate 89 has a Randolph exit three miles NE of the town. The breed of Morgan horses was developed here by Justin Morgan in the early 1800s.

In 1802 **Joseph Smith Sr.** and his wife, **Lucy,** rented out the farm in Tunbridge Gore and moved to the "town" [township] of Randolph, where they ran a **mercantile store** (HJS 32). While here, Lucy became seriously ill with **tuberculosis** and covenanted service to God if she recovered. She did recover, and the family later moved back to the Tunbridge area. Lucy later wrote that, desiring to fulfill her covenant with God, she "went from place to place for the purpose of getting information and finding, if it were possible, some congenial spirit who could enter into my feelings and thus be able to strengthen and assist me in carrying out my resolutions." At that point in her life Lucy was disappointed, concluding that "there was not then upon the earth the religion which I sought" (HJS 33–36).

After merchandising for a short while, Joseph Sr. began crystallizing the wild growing **ginseng root** which sold for a high price in China. A Mr. Stevens took Joseph's ginseng to China, sold it for about $4000, gave nothing to Joseph Sr., then fled to Canada. With a heavy debt of $1800 for store goods, Joseph and Lucy moved back to the **"old farm"** in Tunbridge Gore, which they then sold for $800, half its value. With the money from the sale of their farm and Lucy's wedding gift of $1000 from her brother Stephen and his partner John Mudget, they were able to pay their debts and move to Royalton, then to Sharon (HJS 37–40, 46). The location of the store and their home in Randolph Township is unknown.

Randolph was the birthplace of **Ezra Thayer** on Oct. 14, 1791. Joseph Smith Sr.'s family worked for him in New York. Ezra was called to be one of the missionaries to Missouri in 1831, but he did not go (D&C 32:22). He did fulfill a mission in 1843. After Joseph Smith's martyrdom he did not follow Brigham Young and was eventually baptized into the RLDS Church.

## Other Places of Mormon Interest in Vermont

■ BARRE—**"Granite Center of the World"**

Barre is located six miles SE of Montpelier on U.S. 302. Exit I-89 at Interchange 7 and go east on State 62 for four miles.

At **Barclay's Cutting Establishment,** the 38 ½ foot granite shaft for the **Joseph Smith Monument** was cut, lettered, and polished after being removed from the Marr and Gordon Quarry six miles away. This

*Dunmarr and Gordons Co. at Barre, VT. Cutting a granite stone for the Three Witnesses Monument in Richmond, MO. (Photo by George E. Anderson, 1907; courtesy of LDSCA)*

process took the entire summer of 1905 to complete before the shaft could be sent to Sharon, a distance of about 35 miles. The foundation of the **Hill Cumorah Monument** at Palmyra is also made of granite taken from the quarries at Barre. Also worth visiting in Barre is Graniteville, location of the **Rock of Ages Quarry,** the largest granite quarry in the world. It is located two miles south of Barre just off of State 14.

- **MONTPELIER—The Capital of Vermont**

Montpelier is located near Exit 8 off I-89, six miles NW of Barre.

The **State House** on State Street was dedicated in 1859 and has a dome enhanced with 14-carat gold.

- **PEACHAM**

Peacham is located 10 miles SW of St. Johnsbury. It is on a town road that connects Danville in the north and Groton in the south. This country road is a beautiful drive displaying Vermont's fall foliage around the first week of October.

**Elkins Tavern,** built in 1787, can still be seen on a side road halfway between Peacham and South Peacham. The **Congregational Church** dates from the 1790s. **George B. Harvey,** editor of *Harper's Magazine* and foe of Woodrow Wilson, was born here.

**Lucy Walker Kimball** was born in Peacham on Apr. 30, 1826, and was sealed to the **Prophet Joseph Smith** in 1843. After the death of the Prophet, she became the wife of **Heber C. Kimball,** with whom she had nine children (BiE 1:808–9). She died in Utah on Oct. 1, 1910 (RLDS 37).

- **DANVILLE**

Danville is on U.S. 2, seven miles west of St. Johnsbury. The annual Dowsers Convention is held near Danville for those interested in divining rods. The convention is generally held in August.

**John Boynton,** who became an Apostle in Feb. 1835, stopped for two meetings here while on his mission in the summer of 1834 and baptized seven people (EMS 191:34). At the 1835 St. Johnsbury Conference, presided over by the Twelve, it was recorded that the Danville Branch had 23 members (HC 2:238).

## ■ St. Johnsbury—Birthplace of Erastus Snow and Jacob Gates

St. Johnsbury is located in NE Vermont on U.S. 5 and Interstate 91, seven miles east of Danville at the junction of U.S. 2 and 5.

**Erastus Snow,** son of Levi and Lucina Snow and a member of the Quorum of the Twelve, was born here on Nov. 9, 1818. He believed the testimonies of **Orson Pratt** and **Luke Johnson,** who visited him in 1832, and was baptized in St. Johnsbury by his brother, **William,** Feb. 3, 1833. Of his conversion, Erastus recalled:

*Erastus Snow*

I heard Elder Pratt's message. It seemed to me that it must be true; for from the day he sat at our fireside that evening after his first meeting, while conversing on the scriptures and on the revelations and manifestations to Joseph Smith, the Holy Ghost descended on me, bearing witness that what he was telling was the truth and that they, these Elders, were messengers from God. I began to read the *Book of Mormon,* and so absorbed was I that I felt cheated to have to eat, work, and sleep. I did as Moroni asked me to do, and through the Holy Ghost I did receive the assurance of its truth (ES 2).

Erastus later became a member of the Quorum of the Twelve in 1849 and was engaged in the colonization of the Church in Utah. He died in Salt Lake City on May 22, 1888.

**Jacob Gates,** one of the Presidents of the Seventy from 1862 to 1892, was born here May 9, 1811. He worked on his father's farm during the early period of his life and later worked as a carpenter and joiner. He married **Millie N. Snow** on Mar. 16, 1833. Orson Pratt baptized Gates on June 18, 1833, and **Zerubbabel Snow** confirmed him a member of the Church the same day (BiE 1:103, 111, 115, 197).

In 1830 **Thaddeus Fairbanks,** a storekeeper in St. Johnsbury, invented and patented the world's first **platform scale.** He built a factory here and made a fortune. Fairbanks scales are still manufactured in this city.

At a meeting in Kirtland, OH, on Mar. 12, 1835, the **Prophet Joseph Smith** proposed to the Quorum of the Twelve that they go on their first mission through the Eastern states, holding conferences in various branches of the Church. One such **conference,** called the Vermont Conference, was held in St. Johnsbury on Jul. 17–19, 1835, with the **Twelve** presiding. The boundaries of this conference included the entire state of Vermont and Church branches in Littleton, Dalton, and Landaff in New Hampshire. At this time the St. Johnsbury branch numbered 41 members. On Sunday the l9th, the conference was attended by more than 1,000 people, and nine people were baptized (HC 2:238).

From Saco, ME, **John Boynton,** one of the original **Twelve,** left on a mission to the northern branches to collect funds for the Kirtland Temple. He came to St. Johnsbury to attend a conference attended by numerous elders and high priests who represented seven churches (branches) in the area. He later returned to this town while on the same mission, and after a Sabbath meeting baptized 13 individuals (EMS 191:34).

■ TROY

Troy is located seven miles south of the Canadian border at the intersection of State 100 and 101.

In a letter dated Jan. 23, 1833, **Orson Pratt** states that he preached here and baptized 18 people (EMS 78:33). Orson was one of the first twelve men called to be **Apostles** in 1835.

The nearby Jay Peak Ski Area is a year-round vacation resort with an aerial tramway.

● BORDOVILLE—President Chester A. Arthur Birthplace

Bordoville, the nearest village to the birthplace of **President Chester A. Arthur,** the 21st president of the United States, is located on an unpaved road about five miles south of Enosburg Falls and ½ mile west of State 108. The birthplace is near a country road two miles west of State 108 and 1 ½ miles west of Bordoville. President Arthur's home has been reconstructed.

■ SHELDON—The Birthplace of Heber C. Kimball

Sheldon is on a paved country road 1 ½ miles south of Sheldon Junction and State 105, nine miles directly south of the Canadian border and 10 miles NE of St. Albans.

On Apr. 1, 1799, Solomon and Anna Spaulding Kimball bought 200 acres just north of Sheldon Village near the confluence of Black Creek and the Missisquoi River (HCKM 4–5) and 11 miles from the shores of Lake Champlain.

**Heber C. Kimball,** a member of the original Quorum of the Twelve, was born here on June 14, 1801. The six other siblings in his family were also born here before the Kimballs moved to West Bloomfield, NY, when Heber was about ten years old (TrG 6).

*Heber C. Kimball*

Heber moved with his parents to Bloomfield, NY, in 1811. He then moved to Mendon, NY, in 1820 to work as an apprentice potter with his brother Charles. This move made possible the three most important events in his life: (1) his Nov. 7, 1822, marriage to **Vilate Murray** of neighboring Victor, (2) his acquaintance with Brigham Young, and (3) his acceptance of Mormonism (HCKM 10). In 1831 missionaries of the Church began preaching in Victor, and Heber and a near neighbor, Brigham Young, were baptized in 1832 (T&S 6:471, 488, 503–4). In May 1835 Heber returned to Sheldon as a missionary to preach the gospel to his friends and relatives. Two years later he served a mission to England where he enjoyed tremendous success, paving the way for the growth of the Church in the British Isles for years to come (SLD 117, 119). Elder Kimball served as First Counselor to **President Brigham Young** from 1847 until his death in 1868 (EnM 2:781).

On July 5, 1976, a granite monument was placed at Sheldon in the Sheldon Creek Cemetery in honor of Heber C. Kimball. It was dedicated by **President Spencer W. Kimball,** a great-grandson. The monument is located one mile south of the actual birthplace.

● **GRAND ISLE—Captain Jedediah Hyde Log Cabin**

Located ½ mile NE of Grand Isle on a dirt road off U.S. 2, is the **Hyde Log Cabin,** advertized as the oldest log cabin in the United States. It was built in 1783.

● **BURLINGTON—Ethan Allen's Burial Place**

Burlington, the largest city in Vermont, is on the eastern shore of Lake Champlain on U.S. 7 and I-89.

The **University of Vermont** was founded here in 1791 by Ira Allen, who donated 50 acres of land for the purpose. These acres are now the university campus green.

The handsome **Unitarian Church** at the head of Church Street was built in 1816.

**William H. Russell,** one of the founders of the **pony express,** was a native of Burlington. **Atwater Kent,** a radio manufacturer, was also from Burlington, as was educator **John Dewey.**

**General Ethan Allen's burial place** is located here on Colchester Avenue. In the cemetery is a marble statue erected in honor of this Revolutionary War hero. He led his "Green Mountain Boys" and seized Fort Ticonderoga from the British in May 1775. He was also a noted religious philosopher, writer, and folk hero of Vermont. It is of interest that in 1843 the Prophet Joseph Smith addressed an appeal to "the Green Mountain Boys" of his native state to assist in obtaining redress for the wrongs done to the Saints in Missouri (EnH 911).

Also here is **Battery Park,** the scene of a British naval attack on American fortifications in 1813.

In 1915 there was a little branch of the Church in Burlington.

● ORWELL

Orwell is four miles east of Lake George on State 73 and ½ mile east of State 22A. Being directly opposite Fort Ticonderoga, it was actually a part of the fort and the seat of great military activity during the Revolution.

**Mount Independence** near Orwell is the site of numerous Revolutionary War fortifications. Visitors can see the remains of a stockade, a hospital, a monument, and a fort. Block houses and gun batteries can also be seen here. It received its name because General St. Clair read the American Declaration of Independence to his troops here.

■ BENSON—First Branch in Vermont

Benson is located one mile west of State 22A on county road 141, 14 miles north of Poultney and 50 miles south of Burlington. Benson was the scene of many early religious revivals and spiritual awakenings.

The **first branch** of the Church in the state of Vermont was organized here in 1831 through the efforts of Elder **Jared Carter** (b. 1801). He baptized 27 converts in Benson and witnessed many healings here. Jared's brother, Simeon Carter, stated in a letter to Sidney Rigdon dated Sept. 20, 1832, that a company of Saints, about 30 people, was being persecuted a great deal at Benson when he arrived. By the end of 1832 it was reported that there were over 100 converts in the Church as a result of the Carter brothers' labors (EnH 911). Jared Carter's older brother, Gideon H., was born in Benson, and was killed in the Battle of Crooked River on Oct. 25, 1838 (HC 3:171). **John Boynton** visited this branch while on his mission and baptized one individual.

Of special interest near Benson is a "House with a Past." The house is a renovation and enlargement of an old stone church/schoolhouse. It was built by a small congregation of Free Will Baptists in about 1826. In 1831, mainly through the missionary efforts of Jared Carter, himself a resident of Benson until 1828, most of the Free Will Baptist congregation were converted to The Church of Jesus Christ of Latter-day Saints. The stone church then became the meeting place of the Mormons in Benson until 1833, when the Mormons left Benson to gather with the Saints in Ohio and Missouri.

The building was later used as a schoolhouse until it was abandoned in 1910. It sat empty from 1910 to 1958 when it was purchased by Erick Barnouw, a professor at Columbia University. He bought it at an auction, became intrigued with finding out its past, and eventually remodeled and enlarged it into a lovely home. Erick Barnouw published an account of his searchings and conclusions about the old stone building in a book entitled *House with a Past*. The book also contains interesting details about the early history of the Church in Benson (HWP).

The church/schoolhouse/home is located about five miles from the town of Benson. To find it, travel west on Lake Road from Benson 2.7 miles where the road turns left onto Carter Street. Proceed two miles south on Carter Street, then turn right onto Temple Road (unmarked). One-half mile along Temple Road is the house, on the north side of the road, at the point where Temple Road meets Herrick Road.

■ **POULTNEY—Oliver Cowdery's Residence**

Poultney is near the Vermont-New York border on State 30 and

31, 14 miles straight SW of Rutland. The **Baptist Church** built in 1805 is well preserved, as is the **Eagle Tavern** built in 1790.

From 1826 to 1830 **Horace Greeley** set type in a little printing office in East Poultney as a very young man. He later became a noted journalist, founder of the *New York Herald Tribune,* and founder of the Republican Party. In 1859 Greeley visited Salt Lake City. He spent two hours interviewing Brigham Young, heard Orson Pratt speak in the Tabernacle, and later wrote a book on his travels west which was not complimentary of the Mormons.

The parents of **Oliver Cowdery** moved here with their son in 1809 when he was three. After Oliver's mother died on Sept. 3, 1809, his father remarried (BYUS Summer 1972, p. 414) and Oliver remained here until 1825, when he moved to Manchester, NY (WBM 33). In Manchester he taught school where some of the children of **Joseph Smith Sr.** attended. He met the Smith family and boarded with them for a time. After hearing of Joseph's vision, he left for Harmony, PA, where he met the **Prophet Joseph Smith** and was soon baptized (CHFT 52–53).

■ **WELLS—Birthplace of Oliver Cowdery, Home of Isaac and Elizabeth Hale**

Wells is eight miles south of Poultney on State 30.

**William Cowdery's home site** and foundation are located NE of the Wells town center. A sign near the town library has a map and directions to get to the home site. From the town center, go east on Main Street about .6 mile. Turn north on Saw Mill Road and follow to a fork in the road. Follow the right fork (east) for a short distance to the home site and foundations. The site is identified by a marker on the north side of the road. The marker has a picture of Oliver Cowdery and information about his life.

**Oliver Cowdery,** the youngest of William Cowdery Jr. and Rebecca Fuller's eight children, was born here on Oct. 3, 1806 (CHFT 52–53). He was a third cousin once removed to Joseph Smith (OIC 15). He was involved in a variety of professions in addition to teaching, such as farming, blacksmithing, and clerking. In 1825 he moved to Manchester, NY, where he taught school. On Apr. 7, 1829, Oliver

*Oliver Cowdery (Courtesy of RLDSLA)*

began writing for the **Prophet Joseph Smith** as Joseph translated the plates he had received from the **Angel Moroni** in 1827 (EnM 1:335). Oliver penned almost the entire Book of Mormon twice (the original and a printer's copy). On May 15, 1829, Oliver and Joseph went to the woods to pray to the Lord regarding the practice of baptism. While engaged in prayer they were visited by a heavenly messenger, **John the Baptist,** who conferred upon them the Aaronic Priesthood and instructed them to enter the water and baptize each other, which they did. A short time later Oliver and Joseph received the Melchizedek Priesthood at the hands of **Peter, James, and John.** When the Church was organized on Apr. 6, 1830, in Fayette, NY, Oliver was one of the six original members and was sustained and ordained as an elder of the Church. He was also one of the Three Witnesses of the Book of Mormon, the first General Church Recorder, newspaper editor, and an Assistant President of the Church. In 1832 he married Elizabeth Ann Whitmer in Jackson County, MO. In 1838 he was excommunicated. Following a ten-year estrangement from the Church and a rebaptism in 1848, Oliver planned on going west with the Saints, but he died Mar. 3, 1850 at Richmond, MO, and was buried there before realizing his goal (DCE 109–10). He died in full fellowship in the Church he had helped to establish. He will forever be remembered as a second witness of the Restoration.

The **Isaac Hale home site** is located about 1.8 miles north of the Wells town center on State 30, just east of the highway.

**Isaac Hale** (1763–1839) **(Emma Hale Smith's father),** son of Reuben Hale and Diantha Ward (b. 1741), came from Connecticut to Wells, with his grandfather, Arah Ward, who built the home here. Isaac inherited his grandfather's home. Isaac married **Elizabeth Lewis** in 1767. She was a daughter of Nathaniel Lewis (b. 1740) and Esther Tuttle (b. 1747). Esther was a native of Wells. Isaac took his young wife to the Susquehanna Valley in 1791, the same year Asael Smith moved from Topsfield, MA, to Tunbridge, VT. Elizabeth's brother Nathaniel and his wife, Sarah Cole, went with them. They became the first permanent settlers in the area of present Harmony, PA.

**Emma Hale** was born on July 10, 1804, to Isaac and Elizabeth in Harmony as the third daughter and seventh child of nine (HJS 137). She married Joseph Smith on Jan. 27, 1827, and became the "Elect Lady" as spoken of by the Lord in revelation (D&C 25:3). According to Joseph Smith, the honored designation "Elect Lady" was appropriately realized when Emma was elected as the first president of the Relief Society on Mar. 17, 1842 (HC 4:552–53).

The **Nathaniel Lewis home site** is located in Wells approximately 300 yards north of the Isaac Hale home site (OMN 69).

**Nathaniel Lewis** (b. 1740) married **Esther Tuttle** (b. 1747) in 1767, and after their marriage moved to Wells. Their daughter, **Elizabeth Lewis** (1767–1842), oldest of six children, married Isaac Hale and bore nine children, one of whom was **Emma Hale,** wife of the Prophet Joseph Smith.

■ PAWLET—**Birthplace of George W. Robinson**

Pawlet is located five miles south of Wells on State 30.

**George W. Robinson,** General Church Recorder from 1837 to 1840, was born here in 1814 (KEQR 99).

● RUPERT

Rupert is two miles east of the Vermont-New York border, 6 ½ miles SSW of Pawlet at the intersection of State 153 and 315.

Rupert is the birthplace of **William McClary,** born Oct. 9, 1793. Before July 1838, William married **Sophronia Smith,** sister of the **Prophet Joseph Smith,** after Calvin Stoddard, Sophronia's first husband, died in 1836. William died faithful to the Church sometime before Dec. 8, 1856, and Sophronia became a widow again (MOC 29:1001).

● BENNINGTON

Bennington is located at the intersection of State 9 and U.S. 7 in the SW corner of Vermont.

**The Bennington Battle Monument** is a 306-foot-high stone monolith built in 1891 commemorating American **General John Stark's** Aug. 16, 1777, attack against British **General Burgoyne** during the Revolutionary War.

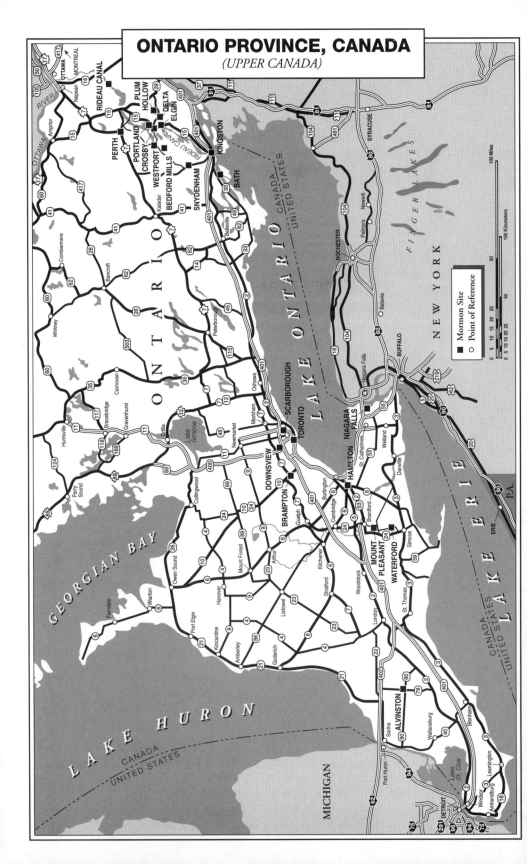

# ONTARIO PROVINCE, CANADA
*(UPPER CANADA)*

**Legend**
■ Mormon Site
○ Point of Reference

# EASTERN CANADA—ONTARIO, QUEBEC, AND THE ATLANTIC PROVINCES

*Larry C. Porter*

୬

FIGHTING BROKE OUT IN THE NEW WORLD BETWEEN the French and the English during the French and Indian War (1756–63). The English objective was to overrun New France and particularly to seize Quebec. However, under the generalship of Louis Joseph de Montcalm-Gozon the routes to Quebec down the St. Lawrence and Lake Ontario were closed to the English. Also British thrusts were successfully stopped at Oswego and Fort Ticonderoga in New York with notable French victories. But the French stronghold at Louisbourg on the St. Lawrence River fell to the British for the second time in 1758. This opened the waterway to Quebec, and in 1759 a fleet of 140 English ships carrying 9,000 British and Colonial American troops sailed up the St. Lawrence and laid siege to the capital of New France. After a lengthy standoff the British, commanded by General James Wolfe, were successful in staging a night landing that led to victory on the Plains of Abraham the next morning. Both Montcalm and Wolfe were killed in the fighting. When the Treaty of Paris brought the greater conflagration of the Seven Years' War (aptly known in the United States as the French and Indian War) to a close in 1763, Great Britain controlled almost the whole of eastern North America.

During the Revolutionary War the rebelling 13 colonies sent two armies north to capture Montreal and Quebec in 1775. Brigadier Richard Montgomery took Montreal, but the combined efforts of Benedict Arnold and Richard Montgomery were not sufficient to capture Quebec. When peace was established in 1783, thousands of United Empire Loyalists, still desirous of

remaining under British rule, left the United States and emigrated to Nova Scotia and the unsettled lands above the St.
Lawrence rapids and north of Lake Ontario. Others, recognizing
the opportunity for land and development, joined that emigration and crossed into the eastern provinces. Emigration from
Europe, primarily from the British Isles, likewise continued to
supply numerous settlers.

The population of Upper Canada remained below the
100,000 level until the War of 1812. But by 1824 the number had
reached close to 150,000, and between 1825 and 1846 the population of British North America expanded to an estimated
450,000 (UC 7). These preliminary events prepared a fertile
proselyting field for Mormon missionaries when the great
Restoration movement began to spread its light abroad under the
direction of the Prophet Joseph Smith in the forepart of the 19th
century.

■ UPPER CANADA (ONTARIO)—Solomon Chamberlin, Fall 1829

Other than his own generalization of **"Upper Canada" (Ontario)**,
we are not certain just where **Solomon Chamberlin** (also spelled
**Chamberlain**) preached to Canadians from loose pages of the
Book of Mormon that he carried into the province in the fall of
1829. This was before the Church was even organized. Solomon
said that he "had occasion to go on a visit into upper Canada." He
was then living at a small settlement called Pilgrimport one mile
NE of the village of Lyons in Wayne County, NY. The Erie Canal at
that time ran directly across the street from his home to the south.
Traveling west along the Erie, he stopped for the night at a farm
house just south of the village of Palmyra, NY. The next morning
the people of the house asked him if he had heard of **Joseph
Smith** and his **Gold Bible.** When he heard the term "Gold Bible,"
Solomon said, "there was a power like electricity went from the
top of my head to the end of my toes." He went to the Smith
home and was instructed from the manuscript of the **Book of
Mormon** for two days by **Hyrum Smith** and others. He was then
taken to the E. B. Grandin printing office in Palmyra and given 64

---

[1] In 1791 the British Parliament enacted the Constitutional Act, whereby Quebec was
split into the two provinces of Upper (Ontario today) and Lower Canada (Quebec
today).

pages of the Book of Mormon that had just been run off the press. Solomon stated: "I took them with their leave and pursued my journey to Canada, and I preached all that I knew concerning Mormonism, to all both high and low, rich and poor, and thus you see this was the first that ever printed Mormonism was preached [in Canada] to this generation. I did not see any one in traveling for 800 miles, that had ever heard of the Gold bible (so called). I exhorted all people to prepare for the great work of God that was now about to come forth, and it would never be brought down nor confounded" (BYUS Spring 1972, pp. 314–17).

Though the **Church** had not yet been organized at Fayette, NY, pages from the still unbound Book of Mormon were being circulated in 1829–30 by such men as Solomon Chamberlin, Joseph Smith, Oliver Cowdery, Martin Harris, and Thomas B. Marsh. Solomon appears to have been the **first person** to **carry** the **message** of the **book** into **Canada,** this during the fall of 1829 (PJE 79–83).

■ KINGSTON/YORK (TORONTO), UPPER CANADA—The Book of Mormon Copyright, Winter 1829–1830

During the winter of 1829–30 the **Prophet Joseph Smith** directed Oliver Cowdery, Joseph Knight, Hiram Page, and Josiah Stowell to **Kingston, Upper Canada,** where they were to investigate the prospects of selling the copyright to the Book of Mormon as an alternative means of financing and publishing the book. B. H. Roberts explained that this meant to "sell the right to publish the book in the Canadian provinces, not dispose of the copyright absolutely" (CHC 1:162). Hiram Page stated that at Kingston they were told that "little **York** [later **Toronto**] was the place where such business had to be done" (Letter of Hiram Page to William E. McLellin, Fishing River, Feb. 2, 1848," RLDS Library-Archives, Independence, MO). David Whitmer mentions only the names of **Oliver Cowdery** and **Hiram Page** as having visited Toronto in the process of events. The endeavor was unsuccessful. This entire episode is very sketchy, but it appears that at an early period these brethren entered Upper Canada (Ontario) on an assigned task. Whether they attempted to preach the content of the manuscript of the Book of Mormon is not stated, but given the opportunity it is unlikely that they would have passed it by (CHC 1:162–63; AAB 30–31).

■ HAMILTON, ONTARIO—**Parley P. Pratt and Moses Nickerson**

The city of **Hamilton** in the regional municipality of Hamilton-Wentworth is situated at the western end of **Lake Ontario,** about 40 miles SW of Toronto. The Queen Elizabeth Way, or QEW, connects the two cities.

In Apr. 1836 **Parley P. Pratt** left his brother **Orson** and **Elder Freeman Nickerson** in the Mount Pleasant area to pursue his missionary appointment to Toronto. As he walked along, he contemplated the long, muddy road to Toronto and the "days of laborious walking" required to get to that city. For the sum of but two dollars he could have taken the time-saving steamboat from Hamilton to Toronto, but he had no money. However, in Hamilton he was able to make contact with **Moses Nickerson,** who provided Parley with ten dollars and a **letter** of **introduction** to **Mr. John Taylor** of **Toronto.** The time-saving steamboat crossing from Hamilton to Toronto was gratefully accomplished on Apr. 19, 1836 (TWP 20–21).

■ MOUNT PLEASANT—**Home of the Nickerson Family**

The village of **Mount Pleasant** is in the township of Brantford, five miles SW of Brantford, near Provincial Highway 24.

The **Prophet Joseph Smith** left Kirtland for Upper Canada (Ontario) on Oct. 5, 1833, for what was to be the first of two visits to Canada. He was accompanied by **Elders Sidney Rigdon** and **Freeman Nickerson.** Arriving at Mount Pleasant on Oct. 18, they were welcomed at the home of Freeman's son, **Eleazer Freeman Nickerson. Moses Chapman Nickerson,** another son, also lived in Mount Pleasant, where the two brothers had opened a shop in 1830. The Prophet and his company preached at Mount Pleasant (in the Nickerson brothers' shop) as well as at **Brantford, Colborne,** and **Waterford** (TWP 14–15).

**Joseph** delivered a simple and forthright message to his listeners, bearing a "faithful testimony that the Priesthood was again restored to the earth, and that God and His Son had conferred upon him the keys of the Aaronic and Melchizedek Priesthoods." He further proclaimed "that the last dispensation had come, and the words of Jesus were now in force—'Go ye into all the world and preach the gospel to every creature. He that believeth and is baptized shall be saved; but he that believeth not shall be damned'" (TWP 15). Many of the people did believe, and the Prophet performed 13 baptisms. One of the converts, **Lydia Bailey,** while yet standing in the waters of baptism, was filled with the Holy Ghost and exclaimed, "Glory to God in the highest! Thanks be to his holy name that I have lived to see this day and be a partaker of this great blessing" (TWP 15). Lydia Bailey later became the wife of widower Newel Knight at Kirtland on Nov. 24, 1835. The Prophet performed the ceremony (TAMF 111–12).

A devotional service was held at the home of Eleazer Freeman Nickerson the evening before the Prophet and his company departed for Kirtland. Seated around the wide, old-fashioned fireplace in the parlor, the family listened attentively to Joseph's discourse. Moses Nickerson voiced the wish that the gift of tongues might be made manifest amongst the newly baptized Saints as it had been anciently, and the Prophet replied, "If one of you will rise up and open your mouth it shall be filled, and you shall speak in tongues." All eyes seemed instinctively to turn towards **Lydia Bailey:** "Sister Lydia, rise up." Lydia did arise and the spirit of tongues came upon her, "and her mouth was filled with the praises of God and His glory." A **branch** of the Church was organized at Mount Pleasant, with Eleazer Freeman Nickerson as the presiding elder. Having set the Church in order here, Presidents Smith and Rigdon returned to Kirtland (TWP 15). For a short time the Mormons met in the **Bathesda Methodist Chapel** in Mount Pleasant (UC 44).

## ■ ALVINSTON—Site of Gardner's Mill

The village of **Alvinston,** Brooke Township, Lambton County, is located on Highway 79, one mile north of Highway 80. Originally called **Gardner's Mill,** the community was not named Alvinston until 1854, when a post office was established. A marker (Marker No. 108) was placed in Alvinston on Aug.

*Millstone from Archibald Gardner's Mill, Alvinston, Brooke Township, Ontario. (1992)*

18, 1946, by the **Utah Pioneer Trails and Landmarks Association** in conjunction with the Ontario members of The Church of Jesus Christ of Latter-day Saints and descendants and relatives of Archibald Gardner. It consists of a stone from the Archibald Gardner Mill and a plaque designating the **"Nauvoo Road"** (Highway 79), which the Gardners and others cut during their exodus in 1846. The monument is located on the west side of Highway 79, .4 mile south of the sign for the Alvinston city limits as you enter the community from the north. The monument is between Lorne and Center Streets, surrounded by a black iron picket fence. The plaque reads as follows:

IN 1846 A GROUP OF CONVERTS TO THE CHURCH OF JESUS CHRIST OF LATTER-DAY SAINTS ENROUTE FROM GARDNER'S MILLS TO NAUVOO, ILL., CHOPPED A ROAD THROUGH THE FOREST TO REACH THE LONDON ROAD. AMONG THEM WAS ARCHIBALD GARDNER THE FIRST SETTLER OF ALVINSTON WHO BUILT THE FIRST GRIST MILL IN BROOKE TOWNSHIP. THE NAUVOO ROAD SANCTIONED AS A BROOKE TOWNSHIP HIGHWAY NOV. 22, 1851, COMPRISES THAT PORTION OF HIGHWAY 79 FROM ROAD ALLOWANCE BETWEEN CONCESSIONS 8 & 9 TO THE NORTHERN TOWNSHIP LINE. THIS STONE FROM GARDNER'S MILL WAS CONTRIBUTED BY THE BROOKE AND ALVINSTON AGRICULTURAL SOCIETY TO WHOM IT WAS PRESENTED BY DUNCAN J. MCEACHERN WHO PROVIDED FOR ITS REMOVAL FROM THE ORIGINAL MILL SITE ON THE EAST BANK OF SYDENHAM RIVER.

In 1837 **Archibald Gardner** constructed a **gristmill** at this site, and the hamlet that grew up around it became known as Gardner's

*Archibald Gardner*

Mill. Archibald then added a sawmill on the east side of **Bear Creek.** During the year of 1843 (1844?) Mormon elders **Thomas, John,** and **Robert Barrowman** came into the area proselyting. John Barrowman preached the gospel to **William Gardner,** brother of Archibald, and he and his family were the first to accept baptism.

**Robert Gardner,** another brother, joined next. He affirmed: "We went about a mile and a half into the woods to find a suitable stream. We cut a hole through ice eighteen inches thick. My brother William baptized me. While under the water, though only a second (it seemed a minute) a bright light shone around my head and my body glowed with warmth." Archibald was taught the gospel by John Barrowman while visiting his brother Robert in Mar. 1845 and was baptized the following April (PION Pt. 1, 54–55; LAG 25–26; UC 73–74).

With the three influential Gardner brothers in the Church, it was not long before there were 25 members in the vicinity. A **branch** was organized by John Barrowman with William Gardner as the branch president (LAG 27). During the winter of 1845–46, **John A. Smith** came to Gardner's Mill and advised the branch membership that the Saints were being driven from Nauvoo and that if they wished to travel west with them they had no time to lose. A Lambton County historian has related the exodus: "[Archibald] Gardner had his mills only a few years when Mormon missionaries converted him. . . . Later in the year 1846, Gardner's family and other converts chopped a road through the bush to London and abandoned their homes to go to Nauvoo. . . . In 1946, one of the stones from Gardner's mill was erected as a monument to them and Gardner beside the Nauvoo Road that they made, now called Highway 79" (UC 74).

The Gardners sold their properties at great personal loss and began their 1,600-mile journey to Nauvoo on Mar. 31, 1846. They crossed the Mississippi River into Lee County, IA, en route to the Rocky Mountains on May 1, 1846 (LAG 28, 33).

■ CHURCHVILLE, ONTARIO—**Home Site of William Law**

**Churchville** is now part of the city of **Brampton** in the regional municipality of Peel. **Brampton** is 8 miles west of metropolitan Toronto on Highway 10. Churchville is situated on the SW side of Brampton near the intersection of Regional Road 1 (Mississauga Rd.) and Regional Road 15 (Steeles Avenue West). From that junction go east on Regional Road 15 for 1.2 miles to Churchville Road. Turn south for ½ mile on Churchville Road to its junction with Church Street on the east side. Churchville has become largely a residential area today. It is located on the Credit River.

**William Law,** later Second Counselor in the **First Presidency** under **Joseph Smith** in Nauvoo (D&C 124:91), and his wife, **Jane Silverthorn,** were converted and baptized in Churchville (then Toronto Township) by **John Taylor** and **Almon W. Babbitt** in 1836.

However, **Samuel Russell** said that it was his father, **Isaac Russell,** who baptized William Law, and in addition, **Wilson Law, Theodore Turley,** and the members of the **Jacob Scott** family living in that same small community (BYUS Winter 1982, pp. 48–49; UC 61–62; CN Jul. 31, 1937).

On Apr. 24, 1837, a **conference** was held at Churchville, which was presided over by **Parley P. Pratt.** Among those present were John Taylor, Isaac Russell, John Snider (also Snyder), Joseph Fielding, and Jacob Scott. William Law was ordained an elder on that occasion and Theodore Turley a priest (M&A 3:511–12).

In Aug. 1837, the **Prophet Joseph Smith** visited Toronto and vicinity and, according to **Joseph Horne,** one of his preaching stops was at Churchville, where William Law was present. William Law later led a **seven-wagon caravan** of Canadian Saints to Nauvoo, arriving in the forepart of Nov. 1839 (LJT 42; BYUS Winter 1982, p. 48; WL 1–3).

■  TORONTO ONTARIO TEMPLE, BRAMPTON

The **Toronto Ontario Temple** is located at 10060 Bramalea Road, **Brampton, ON,** in the NE sector of Brampton, at the junction of Bramalea Road and Bovaird Drive. From Highway 401 West take

Highway 410 north to Bovaird Drive. Go east on Bovaird Drive 1.7 miles to its intersection with Bramalea Road. The temple is on the NW corner of that junction.

During the Church's annual conference on Apr. 7, 1984, the **First Presidency** announced that a **temple** would be

*Toronto Ontario Temple (courtesy of LDSCA)*

built in the **Toronto area.** It was at the organization of the **Kitchener Ontario Stake** by **President Thomas S. Monson** and **Elder M. Russell Ballard** on June 22, 1986, that President Monson identified nearby Brampton as the site for the new temple. **Groundbreaking ceremonies** were conducted by President Thomas S. Monson and Elder M. Russell Ballard on Oct. 10, 1987. President Monson had been president of the **Canadian Mission,** headquartered in Toronto, from 1959 to 1962, while Elder Ballard served as president of the **Canada Toronto Mission** from 1974 to 1976, making the announcement particularly significant to them as well as to countless Canadian Saints (CN Sept. 1, 1990, pp. 3, 6–10).

A grand total of 61,285 individuals toured the beautiful structure during the 16-day **open house** prior to its dedication. **Dedication** of the **Toronto Ontario Temple,** the 44th operating temple, was completed in 11 sessions during a three-day period, Aug. 25–27, 1990. More than 17,000 Saints attended the dedication. The dedicatory services were presided over by Presidents Gordon B. Hinckley and Thomas S. Monson, First and Second Counselors, respectively, in the First Presidency. **President Arnold N. P. Roberts** and his wife, **Audrey,** were called as the **temple president** and **matron.** The temple district included Quebec, New Brunswick, Newfoundland, Nova Scotia, Prince Edward Island, and part of Ontario in Canada, and parts of Michigan, Ohio, Pennsylvania, New York, and Vermont in the United States. Within its confines are located the Prophet's birthplace in Vermont; Palmyra, Manchester, and Fayette, NY; and Kirtland, OH. At a special dinner on Aug. 15, 1990, **Everett S. Pallin,** Church leader and local historian in Toronto, stated, "From the location of the statue of Moroni on the temple [atop the 105-foot spire], I assume we could see Cumorah—the birthplace of the restoration" (CN Sept. 1, 1990, pp. 3, 6–10).

■ DOWNSVIEW, CHARLTON'S SETTLEMENT—**Home of Joseph, Mary, and Mercy Fielding**

**Downsview** is part of the city of **North York,** Municipality of Metropolitan Toronto. The area of interest is NE of the interchange of the MacDonald-Cartier Freeway and Highway 400. The nearest primary intersection is that of Sheppard Avenue and Jane Street. Go south on Jane Street to its intersection with Troutbooke Drive and on the NE portion of that intersection is a public park called **Downsview Dells.** The park is also situated on the east side of Jane Street and just opposite the Oakdale Golf and Country Club, which is on the west. **Black Creek** (running from east to west) is just 85 yards north of the **Downsview Dells** parking lot in a setting open to the public. It was in this vicinity of Black Creek that **Parley P. Pratt** baptized many converts in what was then the area of **Charlton's Settlement.**

**Isabella Russell Walton,** a convert from the city of **Toronto,** made arrangements for **John Taylor** to take **Elder Parley P. Pratt** to meet her brother **Isaac Russell** and his family and friends in the **Downsview** area, which was then called **Charlton's Settlement,** some 9 miles NW of the city of Toronto. A man by the name of **Edward Charlton** had bought property on the SW corner of Keele Street and Sheppard Avenue in 1826. The local preaching appointment for the **Methodist Church** was known as Charlton's Settlement.

After visiting in the home of **Joseph Fielding, Elder Pratt** preached to an attentive audience at the home of **John** and **Francis Russell Dawson.** An appointment was next made to hold a meeting in the **Methodist Meetinghouse,** but as Parley began to speak there were some in the congregation who violently objected. To avoid further contention the meeting was moved to the opposite side of the street on land occupied by Joseph Fielding (TWP 25–26). Here the congregation gathered in a maple grove to hear his sermon. The **Methodist Meetinghouse** was soon opened for further meetings "and in a few days we baptized brother Joseph Fielding and his two amiable and intelligent sisters," **Mary** and **Mercy** (APPP 151–52). The people soon saw the need for baptism by the Lord's authorized servant. **Samuel Russell,** the son of **Isaac Russell,** reported that nearby **Black Creek**

*Mary Fielding Smith, Hyrum Smith's wife and mother of Joseph F. Smith. (Courtesy of LDSCA)*

then became the site of numerous baptisms: "Half a mile west of the meeting house and settlement was a little stream called Black Creek, [and] thither Mr. Pratt repaired, baptizing Isaac Russell and ordaining him an Elder at the water's edge, at the same time and subsequent thereto baptizing Mary Russell, his wife, Frances Russell Dawson and John Dawson, his sister and brother-in-law, their son, William Dawson, and their daughters Margaret, Ruth, and Isabella, John Goodson, Joseph Fielding, his sisters Mary and Mercy Fielding, John Taylor, [Leonora Taylor], John Snider, Margaret and James Wardlaw, Lucy Bridgeland and others" (TWP 25–27; UC 57–59). Isaac Russell was baptized in the latter part of Apr. 1836, while John and Leonora Taylor were baptized on May 21, 1836. Joseph Fielding identified himself and his sisters Mary and Mercy as being among nine who were baptized on May 21, 1836 (TWP 27).

**Orson Pratt** and **Freeman Nickerson** journeyed from **Hamilton, ON,** to work with **Parley** in Charlton's Settlement. **Parley** said that they "organized a branch of the Church, for the people there drank in truth as water, and loved it as they loved life." Joseph Fielding commented that, "all the members in my neighborhood met at my House, as their Sanctuary, until I removed [he moved first to Toronto and then to Kirtland]" (TWP 27–28).

■ TORONTO, ONTARIO—**John and Leonora Taylor**

**Toronto,** situated on the north shore of **Lake Ontario,** is the capital of **Ontario.** To protect their fur trade, the **French** in 1750 established a fortified post here. The **Indians** called it **Toronto,** meaning **"place of meeting."** The land was purchased by the **British** in 1787. **Governor John Graves Simcoe** established **Fort York**

*Leonora Taylor*

*John Taylor*

at the site in 1793. The settlement was named York after the **son of George III of England.** In 1834 the town of York ceased to exist. That year the name reverted back to the original Indian title and the city of **Toronto** was incorporated.

In early Apr. 1836 **Heber C. Kimball** and others made an evening visit to the home of **Parley P. Pratt** in **Kirtland, OH.** Elder Kimball laid hands on **Parley's** head and gave him a **prophetic blessing** saying: "Thou shalt go to Upper Canada, even to the city of Toronto, the capital, and there thou shalt find a people prepared for the fulness of the gospel, and they shall receive thee, and thou shalt organize the Church among them, and it shall spread thence into the regions round about, and many shall be brought to the knowledge of the truth and shall be filled with joy; and from the things growing out of this mission, shall the fulness of the gospel spread into England, and cause a great work to be done in that land" (APPP 130–31).

*Parley P. Pratt*

Parley P. Pratt arrived in Toronto by steamboat from **Hamilton** on Apr. 19, 1836. That same evening he presented himself at the home of **John and Leonora Taylor** bearing a letter of introduction from **Moses Nickerson.** The Taylor home was on the south side of **Newgate Street East (now Adelaide Street),** between Bay and Yonge Streets. He was greeted at the door by Leonora Taylor, who summoned her husband from his wood-turning shop adjoining the house to the rear (the 68-story **Scotia Tower and Plaza,** and the **Bank of Nova Scotia** at 44 King Street West in downtown Toronto now occupy the block which was the site of the Taylor home and shop).[2] He received very little encouragement from the Taylors and spent that night at a public house (APPP 135; UC 56–57).

The next day **Parley visited** the **clergymen** of the city in an attempt to get a place to preach. All of them refused. He appealed to the **sheriff** for the use of the courthouse and then to city authorities for a public room in the marketplace, but to no avail. Parley retired to a grove of pine trees on the outskirts of the city and prayed "in the name of Jesus to open an effectual door for His servant to fulfil his mission in that place" (APPP 135).

Returning to John Taylor's home he intended to pick up some baggage, which he left there, and in doing so spoke briefly with John about his situation. While they were talking, a woman by the name of **Isabella Walton,** a friend of the Taylor's, paid Leonora a visit. Isabella Russell Walton was the widow of the first Lord Chamberlain of the City of Toronto. Upon learning from Leonora of Parley's plight, she declared to Mrs. Taylor: "Tell the stranger he is welcome to my house. I am a widow; but I have a spare room and bed, and food in plenty. He shall have a home at my house, and two large rooms to preach in just when he pleases. . . . I feel by the Spirit that he is a man sent by the Lord with a message which will do us good" (APPP 136).

While living at **Isabella Walton's home** (on Adelaide Street between Toronto and Yonge Streets) Elder Pratt was invited to join a **Methodist study group** to which Sister Walton and the Taylors belonged. It was held at the home of **Mr. William P. Patrick** on Bay Street. **Parley** was invited to give a series of responses in these gatherings. However Mr. Patrick soon became alarmed at the

---

[2] Bishop Everett S. Pallin, local historian, introduced me to the site of the Taylor home and wood-turning shop and other key historical locations in the Toronto area on Aug. 25, 1986.

direction taken and refused to open his home to any further discussions by the elder. Parley's discourses were continued at the Walton residence. Isabella Russell Walton, a native of **Liverpool, England,** was among the **first** to be **baptized,** along with her sister **Sarah Russell Cavanaugh** and her niece **Ann Wanlass,** in the waters of **Toronto Bay** (TWP 24). Sister Walton arranged for Elder Pratt to visit with her brother **Isaac Russell** and others in nearby **Downsview** in an area known as Charlton's Settlement, where he enjoyed marvelous success in his proselyting.

Elder Parley Pratt soon required assistance in his labors, and his brother **Orson Pratt** in company with **Freemen Nickerson** took passage by steamboat from **Hamilton to Toronto** on May 20, 1836. Orson Pratt preached in the **Walton Home** and also in that of **John Snider,** who was a brickmaker and mason on Berkeley Street. Parley left the area in May 1836 for **Kirtland** and when he returned in June, he brought his wife, **Thankful Halsey Pratt,** to share in his missionary experience. The Pratts returned to Kirtland in the autumn of 1836 and were there for the arrival of their son, **Parley P. Pratt Jr.,** born on Mar. 25, 1837. Sadly, **Thankful died** within three hours of the birth of her son. Soon after her departure, a very lonesome Parley returned to Toronto in the spring of 1837. While here he conferred with the Saints on the "subject of a mission to England." At length, **Joseph Fielding** (who had already immigrated to Kirtland), **Isaac Russell, John Goodson,** and **John Snider,** were selected from among the Canadian brethren to go along with **Heber C. Kimball, Orson Hyde,** and **Willard Richards** to the British Isles. The elders from Canada were an essential and effectual door to the opening of the missionary labor in Great Britain (TWP 27–29, 38–43; APPP 165–68).

The **Prophet Joseph Smith, Sidney Rigdon,** and **Thomas B. Marsh** came to **Toronto** in Aug. 1837. **John Taylor** had been appointed to preside when the Apostles (Parley P. Pratt and Orson Hyde, who had joined Parley in July 1836) left the Toronto area in the autumn of 1836. Elder Taylor now had the grand experience of accompanying the Prophet and his associates in visiting the churches. John declared, "This was as great a treat to me as I ever enjoyed. . . . I had daily opportunity of conversing with them, of listening to their instructions, and in participating in the rich stores of intelligence that flowed continually from the Prophet Joseph." Prior to leaving Canada, the Brethren ordained John Taylor a high priest on Aug. 21, 1837, and reaffirmed his appointment to preside over the branches of the Church (LJT 42–44).

**Theodore Turley,** laboring in the Toronto area, converted **Samuel Mulliner** on Sept. 10, 1837. Samuel was born in **Haddington, East Lothian, Scotland.** He and a fellow Scot, **Alexander Wright,** born in **Marnoch,** near **Banff, Banffshire,** and converted in **Canada** in 1836, were the **first missionaries** to serve in **Scotland.** They arrived in **Glasgow, Scotland,** on Dec. 20, 1839 (TWP 28, 268).

■ SCARBOROUGH—**Site of Orson Hyde's Debate with a Sectarian Minister**

Once a small settlement in **Scarborough Township,** bounded on the south by Lake Ontario, **Scarborough** is now a city to the NE of metropolitan Toronto. The **Scarborough Civic Center** is located SW of Exit 381 on Highway 401 (MacDonald-Cartier Freeway).

**Elder Orson Hyde** joined Parley P. Pratt in Toronto during July 1836. He arrived just in time to be involved in a public debate in nearby **Scarborough.** The two missionaries were challenged to **debate** the scriptural validity of the doctrine they were preaching by a learned **Presbyterian clergyman** named **Browning.** Just at the appointed time of the debate Parley was called back to testify in a **Kirtland** court case and had to leave Orson to "meet the champion alone." As there was no building large enough to hold the crowd, it was decided to meet in the open air. A grove of trees supplied the needed space. However, when the hour arrived, Elder Hyde faced a different divine, one **Mr. Jenkins,** who had replaced **Browning.** Orson remembered that his opponent, "came with some less than a mule-load of books, pamphlets and newspapers, containing all the slang of an unbelieving world" (TWP 29).

In his opening statement Elder Hyde laid down the **principles** by which the **Church of Jesus Christ** could be **recognized,** as outlined in the **Bible:** "A true Church of Christ is composed of apostles, prophets, elders, teachers and members, who have been baptized [by immersion] in the name of Jesus Christ, and who have received his spirit by the laying on of hands of his apostles, or authorized servants.

"A true Church of Christ believed in visions, angels, spirits, prophesyings, revelations, healings and miracles of every kind, as described in the New Testament. Any creed or religious body differing from this New Testament pattern could not be considered the Church of Christ, however sincere they might be" (APPP 156).

Elder Hyde then called upon his opponent to confirm or deny these premises. Recognizing the implications, Mr. Jenkins would neither confirm nor deny them. At the conclusion of several exchanges, Orson stated: "The enemy's fire soon became less and less spirited, until, at length, under a well directed and murderous fire from the long "eighteens" with which Zion's fortress is ever mounted—to wit: the Spirit of God—the enemy raised his hand to heaven and exclaimed, with affected contempt, "Abominable! I have heard enough of such stuff." I immediately rejoined, "Gentlemen and ladies, I should consider it highly dishonorable to continue to beat my antagonist after he had cried enough" (TWP 30). Approximately 40 individuals were baptized into the Church in that vicinity immediately following the debate (TWP 30).

■ **ERNESTOWN (ALSO EARNESTOWN)—First Branch in British North America**

**Ernestown** is a township in **Leonnox and Addington County.** It is situated along the North Channel of **Lake Ontario.** The village of **Bath** lies within the township, and is located on Highway 33 about 15 miles SW of the city of **Kingston,** on Lake Ontario. Ernestown was surveyed in 1783, and is named in honor of **Ernest,** the eighth child of **King George III** of **England.** It was settled in 1784 by **United Empire loyalists.** On Aug. 9, 1997, Saints of the **Trenton District, Canada Toronto East Mission,** commemorated the Church's sesquicentennial remembrance of the pioneers in the Salt Lake Valley (1847–1997), and likewise celebrated more than 150 years of their own Ontario heritage. Carma T. Prete chaired the sesquicentennial committee. **President Thomas S. Monson** of the First Presidency and former president of the Canadian Mission dedicated a seven-foot stone monument with an appropriate plaque to the early missionaries and Saints of this land. The historical marker is located in the village of **Bath** at **Finkle's Shore Park** (CN Aug. 16, 1997, pp. 3, 8).

Early in June 1832, **Joseph and Phineas Young** from the Mendon/Victor area of New York, and **Elders Elial Strong, Eleazer Miller,** and **Enos Curtis** of Bradford and Tioga Counties, PA, journeyed to Ernestown to proselyte. They arrived just at the close of the yearly conference of the **Methodist Reformed Church,** and attended its quarterly meeting. **Phineas** had formerly been a member of that denomination and just two years previous had preached in the very meetinghouse where they were gathered. The **Methodists** knew that Phineas had become a **Mormon** and very reluctantly granted him the privilege of preaching in that house at five in the evening. Phineas reported, "I had a full house and good liberty, and at the close of my meeting I had more invitations to preach than I could attend to" (MS 25:376). He and his companions labored in the area for about six weeks. They were successful in establishing the **first branch in British America** (MS 25:376; see also TGCM 4–5).

In reporting their labors, **Elial Strong** and **Eleazer Miller** declared, "Here [Ernestown and vicinity], thousands flocked to hear the strange news; even so that the houses could not contain the multitude, and we had to repair to groves. Hundreds were searching the scriptures to see if these things were so. Many were partly convinced and some were wholly so" (HCC 17; EMS May 1833). Among the converts responding to the message of this first group of missionaries were James and Philomela Smith Lake and their extended family. James had lost a leg but despite this handicap was able to aid in the construction of the Kirtland and Nauvoo Temples, and after coming to Utah was ordained as a stake patriarch. He was buried in Oxford, ID, in 1873. Philomela is buried beside him (ZSCF 7; BiE 2:387–88).

**Brigham Young** embarked on a **second mission** into **Upper Canada** in the spring of 1833. An early resident in the area, **Peter Bristol** of **Napanee Township,** recalled that, "There was quite an excitement in the county [Addington] over the Mormon missionaries who went about the different townships Bath, Earnestown, Fredericksburg preaching and baptizing converts. Quite a number were baptized in Big Creek. Brigham Young was here himself; and if I remember aright, he preached at Bath" (UC 39).

Among the converts from **Ernestown** was **Artemus Millet,** who followed the trade of a mason. Although he lived in Ernestown, he was baptized at **Loughborough** by **Brigham Young** on Feb. 18, 1833 [also stated as Jan. 1833]. **Joseph Young** had apparently known Artemus previously, and informed the **Prophet Joseph Smith** of his potential assistance in building the **Kirtland Temple** as plans were being laid for the construction of that house. The **Prophet** is reported to have stated to **Joseph** and **Brigham Young,** "I give you a mission to go and baptize him into the church and tell him to bring $1,000 with him" (CN Aug. 30, 1975, p. 16). Another account specified that **Lorenzo D. Young** informed the Prophet of the Canadian convert's skills and that Artemus subsequently visited Kirtland as requested in a letter from **Hyrum Smith.** At that time Artemus had 36 Scottish masons employed in his business and had contracted to build bridges for the British government. Nevertheless, he turned the business over to family members, went to Kirtland and began work on the temple. Returning to Canada, he settled his business and brought his household to Kirtland. **Artemus** supervised the selection of **stones** and the **exterior masonry work,** including the remarkably hard and **beautiful plaster,** or stucco, that shown in the sun because of the broken glassware placed in it (HeR 150–51; CN Dec. 31, 1977, p. 12; BYAM 51).

- **SYDENHAM (ONCE LOUGHBOROUGH), LOUGHBOROUGH TOWNSHIP, FRONTENAC COUNTY, ONTARIO—Home of Daniel Wood, Progenitor of Pres. Henry D. Moyle**

The settlement of **Loughborough** in **Loughborough Township** changed its name to **Sydenham** in 1883, for Lord Sydenham, Governor-in-Chief of Canada. It is located 16 miles NW of **Kingston** in the southwestern part of **Frontenac County.** The 1826 home of

*Daniel Wood Home, Sydenham, Ontario*

**Daniel Wood,** early Mormon convert, still stands in Sydenham near the north shore of **Sydenham Lake** on the south side of **Bedford Road.** The large 2 ½ story limestone home is set back ¼ mile from the street and it is difficult to see it plainly from the road. *Please note: this is private property and the present owners have specifically asked that their privacy not be disturbed by anyone.* The home is plainly visible from the vantage point of the lakeside park on the east side of the village of Sydenham and the south edge of Lake Sydenham. Look north across the lake and you can readily see the house standing "on a ridge surrounded by trees, with lawns sloping down to the water's edge" (CTP Jan. 2, 1997). Brigham Young and Joseph Young preached in this house.

In Dec. 1832 Brigham Young and his brother Joseph came to **Upper Canada** from **Mendon, NY**. Passing through **Kingston** they proceeded to **West Loughborough** (now **Sydenham**). Here they spent one month preaching in the vicinity. They succeeded in baptizing some 45 persons (MHBY 5). **Daniel Wood** said that he and some of his **neighbors** had previously met with **Mormon elders** in his house earlier in 1832, "but they [the elders] left before any of us were baptised" (these were the missionaries from the Mendon/Victor area of NY and Bradford and Tioga Counties in PA). Meanwhile, Daniel and his friends had continued to study the scriptures and were praying about them when Elders Brigham and Joseph Young visited them. Daniel recorded that the "two Brothers came and preached to us and showed us more perfectly the order of the Church of Christ then we all with one accord went forth and was rebaptised [they had been previously baptized by a Reformed Methodist, Mr. Robert Perry] by one who had been called and ordained to administer in the ordinances of the house of God" (JDW 2). Daniel and his wife, Mary Snider, were baptized by Brigham Young on Feb. 17, 1833 (TFBR 260–61).

Significantly, within **Daniel Wood's posterity** was a great-grandson, **Elder Henry D. Moyle,** who served as both second and first counselor to **President David O. McKay** in the First Presidency (ZSCF 8). **Woods Cross, UT,** is named after **Daniel Wood** (UHE 642). Daniel died in Woods Cross on Apr. 15, 1892, and is buried in "his little private Cemetery," the Wood Cemetery, Bountiful, UT (TFBR 261).

*Henry D. Moyle,*
*Apostle*

**Daniel Wood's grandson Wilford C. Wood** of Woods Cross, UT, was a great benefactor to the members of the Church because of his **preservation of Church historical sites.** He spent much of his lifetime gathering historical properties and items that pertained to the Prophet Joseph Smith. He purchased the Liberty Jail site, land at Adam-ondi-Ahman, the John Johnson House and farm in Hiram, OH, the Newel K. Whitney Store in Kirtland, OH, seven plots of the Nauvoo Temple site, and Church-related properties in Harmony Township, PA. His timely procurement of these holdings and acquisition of numerous documents and artifacts associated with

*Wilford C. Wood, Benefactor and Preserver (courtesy of Wilford C. Wood)*

the Restoration has saved these invaluable resources from being misused, lost, or even destroyed by persons not having a true regard for their historical significance. Our sincere thanks to Wilford C. Wood!

The missionaries organized a **branch** at **West Loughborough** along with some other branches in the area. Then they returned to Mendon, NY, in Feb. 1833 (UC 38; TWP 14).

**Brigham Young** returned to that same mission field again in Apr. 1833, accompanied by a young priest from the Lyons New York Branch named **Jonathan Hampton** (MHBY 6; It is not certain just how long Jonathan stayed with Brigham Young following their departure from Lyons). After proselyting in **Theresa,** and Indian River Falls, NY, Elder Young went by steamboat from Ogdensburg, St. Lawrence County, NY, to **Kingston,** then on to **Ernestown.** From here Brigham Young directed successful labors in Ernestown, West Loughborough, Fredericksburg Township, and in the area of **Napanee** (MHBY 6; ZSCF 8).

In July 1833 Brigham Young gathered up a number of convert families for a move to Kirtland, OH. Among those making up the company were brothers **Daniel** and **Abraham Wood** of Loughborough (Sydenham today), and **James Lake** and his son **Dennis,** who lived in Camden to the north of Ernestown. Brigham Young escorted them to Kirtland. It was **one of the earliest Canadian emigrations** in response to the **doctrine of gathering** (JH Apr. 1, 1833; TWP 14).

During the years 1832 to 1834, about 150 converts embraced Mormonism in that area. **Branches** were organized in Loughborough Township, West Loughborough (Sydenham), Ernestown, and Kingston (UC 39). When the **Quorum of the Twelve Apostles** took a united mission to the Eastern States and Canada, six members of the Twelve visited West Loughborough and held a conference here on June 29, 1835: **David W. Patten, Heber C. Kimball, Luke S. Johnson, Orson Pratt, John F. Boynton,** and **Lyman E. Johnson. Elder Frederick M. Van Leuven** was appointed to preside over the branch (UC 40; HCM June 29, 1835).

■ Kingston, Frontenac County

The historic city of **Kings Town** (soon shortened to **Kingston**), was named after **George III,** by **United Empire loyalists,** who settled here in the 1780s. It is situated on Highways 2 and 401, on the NE shore of **Lake Ontario.** The **Rideau Canal,** constructed between 1826 and 1832 as a military route to **Bytown (Ottawa),** begins here.

In Aug. 1830, **Phineas H. Young** accompanied his brother **Joseph Young** on his return from Mendon, NY, to Upper Canada, where Joseph had been laboring as a minister for the **Reformed Methodists.** On their way they stopped at the home of a former Reformed Methodist who had been converted to Mormonism, **Solomon Chamberlin.** He was living in the small rural settlement of **Pilgrimport, Lyons Township, NY.** Solomon preached to the two brothers from the **Book of Mormon.** Continuing their journey they passed through **Kingston** before arriving at **Ernestown,** where they began to labor. Phineas couldn't get the Book of Mormon out of his mind and soon decided to return home. On his way he attended a quarterly meeting of the **Episcopal Methodists** at Kingston, and that evening at his hotel he found many of the Methodists assembled in two large rooms. Greatly moved by the spirit that was working in him, **Phineas** stood in the doorway between the two rooms and requested the attention of the group, which numbered about 100 persons. Having asked if anyone present had read the **Book of Mormon,** he was invited to enlighten them. Phineas reported: "I commenced by telling them that it was a revelation from God, translated from the Reformed Egyptian language by Joseph Smith, jun., by the gift and power of God, and gave a full account of the aborigines of our country, and agreed with many of their traditions, of which we had been hearing this evening. . . . I bore a powerful testimony to the work, and thus closed my remarks and went to bed, not to sleep, but to ponder with amazement at the power that seemed to compel me thus to speak" (MHBY xix-xxii). This account by Phineas is one of the earliest references to a discourse on Mormonism being presented in Upper Canada.

That same month, Aug. 1830, **Joseph Smith Sr.** and his son **Don Carlos Smith** journeyed from the **Palmyra** area to visit Joseph Sr.'s father, **Asael Smith Sr.** in **East Stockholm, St. Lawrence County, NY.** The **Prophet** said that his father touched "on his route at several of the Canadian ports [on the north shore of Lake Ontario and/or along the St. Lawrence River], where he distributed a few copies of the Book of Mormon" (HC 4:190). It is likely that **Kingston** was one of those **"Canadian ports,"** although not explicitly stated.

After a visit with the members of the Columbia Pennsylvania Branch of the Church in January 1832, the as yet **unbaptized Brigham Young** was anxious to share a knowledge of the principles that he had learned with his brother **Joseph Young,** who was preaching for the **Methodist Reformed Church** in the vicinity of **Kingston.** Recalling his journey by horse and sleigh, on which he was accompanied as far as **Sackets Harbor** by **John P. Greene,** Brigham said that "After finding my brother Joseph, and explaining to him what I had learned of the Gospel in its purity, his heart rejoiced, and he returned home with me, where we arrived in March [1832]" (MHBY 2).

**Joseph** and **Phineas Young, Eleazer Miller, Enos Curtis, Elial Strong,** and another unnamed missionary came through **Kingston** and labored in the greater area in June 1832. When the other elders elected to return to the United States in July 1832, Joseph Young chose to remain in the vicinity of Kingston until the following September and organized a second branch of the Church (the first branch was in **Loughborough;** ZSCF 7).

In Dec. 1832 **Brigham Young** accompanied his brother **Joseph** to **Upper Canada.** This was Brigham Young's **first mission into Canada.** Starting from Mendon, NY, they walked through mud and deep snow until they reached Gravelly Point, NY, on **Lake Ontario.** There they made a six-mile crossing on the ice to the town of Kingston. Brigham later recalled that "the ice was very thin and bent under our feet, so that in places the water was half shoe deep, and we had to separate from each other, the ice not being capable of holding us." From Kingston the missionaries proceeded on to **West Loughborough** (TWP 14).

During the autumn of 1836, **Parley P. Pratt** was encouraged by the Saints in Toronto to go to Kingston and meet the **Irvingite preacher William R. Caird.** It was hoped that the two men would form an amicable relationship. With **John Goodson** as a companion, Parley took the steamer to Kingston in hopes of finding some common grounds for discussion with Mr. Caird. However, Parley was **not granted an interview.** Rather, Caird chose to **rail against Mormonism** and when Elder Pratt tried to speak in defense of the

Saints in a public meeting where Caird was preaching, he was denied the privilege (TWP 30–31).

In 1837 the call was issued for certain **Canadian brethren** to join **Heber C. Kimball** and other Kirtland missionaries in **New York City** to go on an extended mission to **Great Britain.** During June **Elder John Goodson** and **priests Isaac Russell** and **John Snider** from the Toronto area gathered in Kingston prior to crossing into the United States. Also traveling with them as far as Schenectady, NY, were **Elders Wilford Woodruff, Jonathan H. Hale, and Milton Holmes,** who were continuing their missionary labors in the **eastern United States** (TWP 38–39; JWW 1:153–54).

Under the date of May 15, 1841, the **Prophet Joseph Smith** reported that good news had recently been received from **Canada. Elders John Morrison** and **[Ormus E.?] Bates** had performed **20 baptisms** in Kingston (JH May 15, 1841).

■ RIDEAU CANAL—Missionary Waterway

From Lake Ontario at Kingston, the **Rideau Canal** begins its ascent of the **Cataraqui River** system. At **Kingston Mills** boats pass through the first of a fleet of locks and waterways which ultimately lead 120 miles to **Ottawa** (originally **Bytown**). In 1826 England sent **Lieutenant Colonel John By** of the **Royal Engineers** to supervise the construction of the canal. It was to be a secure water route to allow troops and supplies from **Montreal** to reach the settlements of **Upper Canada** and the strategic naval facilities at **Kingston,** should there be new hostilities between Canada and the United States. It was completed in 1832. When threats of war never materialized it soon became a major artery for regional commerce.

The **Rideau Canal** proved a ready route for the early **Mormon missionaries,** who were proselyting in the region. **Elders Wilford Woodruff, Jonathan Hale,** and **Milton Holmes** arrived at Kingston from Sackets Harbor, NY, on June 6, 1837, and walked the six miles NE to **Kingston Mills** on July 7, where they spent the night. The next morning they took steamboat passage up the Rideau Canal as far as the locks at **Jones Falls.** They then walked to Brother **Artemus Judd's** place in the township of **Bastard, Leeds.** The visiting elders participated in a conference of the churches in the area. While in that vicinity they called on a **Sister Carnes,** who had two sick children. **Elder Woodruff** declared, "One was a suckling child. Lay at the point of death. I took it in my arms. Presented it before the Elders. They lade their hands upon it while in my arms & and we healed it in the name of Jesus Christ & returned it whole to its Mother. The other Child was also healed" (JWW 1:150–53).

■ **LEEDS-GRENVILLE COUNTY**

Today the counties of **Leeds** and **Grenville** are united for municipal purposes, and **Brockville** (formerly **Elizabethtown**) is the county seat. Brockville is located in Leeds County in eastern Ontario Province on the St. Lawrence River. The McDonald-Cartier Freeway, Highway 401, provides ease of access.

■ **ELDER JOHN E. PAGE**

No Canadian missionary enjoyed more success in his proselyting than **Elder John E. Page.** At the time of his call by the **Prophet Joseph Smith,** John observed that it would be difficult for him to go as he "was destitute of clothing." The Prophet took off his own coat and gave it to him with the admonition to "go, and the Lord would bless him abundantly on his mission" (MS 27:103). Elder Page departed Kirtland in company with **Elder William Harris** on May 31, 1836. They first began their labors in the township of **Loughborough, Frontenac County,** where they added 14 members to that branch.

■ **PROSELYTING IN LEEDS-GRENVILLE COUNTY**

After leaving **Loughborough, Elder Page** recounted, "we traveled to Leed's Church, distance 20 miles, and baptised 3.—From thence we traveled 25 miles to Bedford [Frontenac County], and North Crosby [Leeds-Grenville County], where we planted a church that now numbers 68 members" (M&A 3:446). Having unitedly baptized some 40 converts in all, **Elder William Harris** concluded to leave the field on Sept. 5, 1836, and journey to **Missouri.** Alone, Elder Page labored in **South Crosby** and **Bastard Townships.** To his "great joy" **Elder James Blakesley** joined him in the ministry on Sept. 25, 1836. Together they baptized 97 people before Elder Blakesley also took his leave on Nov. 17, 1836. Working incessantly, and again alone, John baptized an additional 41 persons by Jan. 1, 1837. Elder Page stated, "of this number 19 belong in and about the village of Perth, U.C. 20 miles or more from Bastard and South Crosby branches. Besides all this the elders and priests who have been ordained at the conferences I have held have swelled the number of those baptized to 267 in all added to the church in the bounds of the territory where I have labored over seven months" (M&A 3:446). His labors during this time also carried him to the **Elgin, Westport,** and **Portland** areas. John E. Page then returned to Kirtland, concluding his **first mission** to **Upper Canada** (UC 46–47).

On Feb. 16, 1837, Elder Page again left Kirtland with his wife and two children for a **second mission** to Upper Canada. Some 400 new converts were reaped as he strengthened the members and established new branches in the township areas of **Bedford, Bathurst, North** and **East Bathurst, Leeds, Williamsburg, Bastard,** and **West Bastard.** Under the direction of the Spirit, Elder Page was responsible for the **baptisms** of upwards of **600 souls** in his combined missions to Leeds County (UC 47; BiE 1:92).

■  BASTARD TOWNSHIP, LEEDS—**Birthplace of President Gordon B. Hinckley's Grandfather Ira Nathaniel Hinckley**

**Bastard** and **South Burgess Township** (united in 1849 for municipal purposes), is situated west of **Brockville.** The town hall is located 3.6 miles NE of the village of **Philipsville** in the small rural community of **Chantry.** The primary village communities today are Delta, Plum Hollow, Philipsville, Chantry, Harlem, Forfar, Newboyne, and Portland.

*President Gordon B. Hinckley*

It is of particular interest today that among those persons attracted to the gospel by the efforts of Elder John E. Page and his companions were the progenitors of **President Gordon B. Hinckley.** On Aug. 8, 1998 Pres. Gordon B. Hinckley spoke to the Saints in Hamilton, ON. He explained that his great-grandfather, Nathaniel Hinckley, had died in eastern Canada in an early day (died, Bastard, Leeds, ON, Canada, Sept. 8, 1831, see AHIH 743). He informed the congregation, "Three days ago, I stood at what we presume to be his grave in that part of the country. I walked out through a cow pasture to get to it, to find it. It is a little fenced-in cemetery there, and I had a thousand feelings of reverence and respect and gratitude and thanksgiving" (CN Aug. 15, 1998, p. 3).

*Ira Nathaniel Hinckley and Angeline Wilcox Noble Hinckley, President Gordon B. Hinckley's paternal grandparents.*

The **Nathaniel** and **Lois Judd Hinckley** family reportedly lived in the **Plum Hollow** area, 6½ miles east of Philipsville (HJ Aug. 13, 1992). **Arza Erastus Hinckley** and his younger brother **Ira Nathaniel Hinckley** (the latter being the **grandfather** of President Gordon B. Hinckley) were born in the township of Bastard,

Leeds County, on Aug. 15, 1827, and Oct. 30, 1828, respectively. When their father, Nathaniel Hinckley (also Erastus Nathaniel Hinckley), became too seriously ill to take care of the family, Arza, still a small child, was placed in the home of his maternal grandfather, Arza Judd Sr., while Ira, who was not yet two years old, remained at home with his mother, Lois Judd Hinckley. Their father died at age 35 of tuberculosis on Sept. 8, 1831. Four years later Lois married **Evi Judd.** In the summer of 1836 members of both the Judd and Hinckley families were proselyted to and converted by Elders John E. Page and James Blakesley (TWP 17–18; AHIH 1, 9; BiE 1:92).

During the fall and winter of 1837–38, Elder John E. Page organized a company of Saints referred to as the **"Canada Camp,"** with a design to escape the "Rebellion of Upper Canada" (UC 23, 61–64) and also to begin the long journey to gather with the Saints in northern Missouri. Some elements of the company began to assemble on the United States side of the border in St. Lawrence County during the later part of 1837. Arza Erastus Hinckley remembered 1837 as the time of crossing with his family (AHIH 9). However, the majority did not leave their homes until January 1838 when "over 200 vehicles carrying men, women and children departed from Elgin [South Crosby Township, Upper Canada]" and moved across the border. It was said that this "caravan of Canadian emigrants crossed the St. Lawrence River at Cole's Ferry" and that "they arrived at Oak Point in St. Lawrence County, NY, to prepare for a spring departure" (ZSCF 13). Travel times and routes varied for groups leaving from this departure point. Some journeyed to Kirtland, OH, by water across Lakes Ontario and Erie. Others traveled overland and drove the company's cattle. There were those who apparently went very early in the spring of 1838. By March, for instance, **Joel Judd** was subscribing to the constitution of Kirtland Camp, a travelling company organized by the Seventy in Kirtland.

The principal company of Kirtland-bound Saints left Oak Point and vicinity on May 14, 1838, under John E. Page's personal direction. There were some few who gave up entirely and remained behind (ZSCF 13–14). The Judd-Hinckley families stayed briefly in Kirtland and were subsequently part of the John E. Page Company as it traveled from Kirtland to Missouri. Arza E. Hinckley was baptized by Lyman Stoddard while crossing through Illinois on Aug. 15, 1838, en route to Missouri (AHIH 9; BiE 4:746). Ira Nathaniel Hinckley, grandfather of President Gordon B. Hinckley, was later baptized on July 1, 1843, during the Illinois period. The whole family was eventually united together in Illinois after a period of separation. Some members of the Judd and Hinckley families were residing in the Mormon settlement of De Witt, Carroll County, MO, by Oct. 1838. Unfortunately their arrival coincided with the attack and siege of De Witt by a vicious mob. Forced to surrender, the inhabitants made their way to Far West, Caldwell County, MO. In northern Missouri the persecution continued until the Saints were expelled from the state by the extermination order of Governor Lilburn W. Boggs. Members of the Judd and Hinckley families were among the exiles who found a new home and momentary safety in the state of Illinois (TWP 17–18; AHIH 1, 9; BiE 1:92; EDH Nov. 21, 1996).

■ WILFORD WOODRUFF IN LEEDS

**Elder Wilford Woodruff** arrived in **Bastard Township** on June 8, 1838, and stayed with **Artemus Judd.** On the tenth he met in conference with **Elders John E. Page** and **James Blakesley** and with members representing some 300 Saints and eight branches of the Church. Elder Woodruff recorded, "It was with peculiar feelings that I arose to address a large Congregation of Saints raised up in another nation under an other Government seperate from mine own nation for this was the first time that I arose to address a congregation of Saints under the British government" (JWW 1:151–52).

■ **MONTREAL AND QUEBEC**

**Montreal,** capital of the **Province of Quebec,** is located on Quebec Autoroute 40 in the southern end of the province. The city itself is situated on a large island in the **St. Lawrence River.** Next to Paris, France, Montreal is the **largest French-speaking city** in the world. The city of Quebec is situated in SE Quebec Province on a steep-sided cliff, which rises 360 feet above the St. Lawrence River. Quebec Autoroute 40 accesses the city. **Ninety-five percent** of its populace speaks French.

In Nauvoo on May 20, 1843, Elders Jesse W. Crosby and **Benjamin Brown** were assigned to preach the gospel in Nova Scotia (HC 5:413). Elder Crosby described their brief proselyting experience in the cities of Montreal and Quebec on the way to their appointment: "In August, 1843, Elder Benjamin Brown and myself, having been appointed to visit the British Provinces, proceeded to western New York, where we spent the Winter. We organized several branches of the Church, and baptized upwards of 150 souls, and held two conferences. After tarrying eight months, we went to Montreal and Quebec [in 1844], making a short stay in each of these Catholic cities, preached some and circulated some books, pamphlets, etc. Thence we proceeded down the St. Lawrence twenty five miles below Quebec, thence crossing over to New Brunswick" (JH Nov. 19, 1844).

Because of the language barrier, the earliest missionaries of the restoration primarily bypassed these French-speaking cities in their proselyting.

■ **POTTON TOWNSHIP, BROME COUNTY**

**Potton Township** is located in **Brome County** (originally **Stanstead County**), Quebec Province (then termed **Lower Canada**). The township's southern boundary is on the Canada-United States line between Brome County, PQ and Orleans County, VT, and it lies on the west side of **Lac Memphremagog.** The principal community in the township is **Masonville** on Highway 243 in south-central Potton Township.

What appears to be the **earliest missionary effort** in Lower Canada (Quebec) was begun by **Elder Orson Pratt** in 1833. He left Charleston, VT, on July 19, and on the 20th was preaching in the township of Potton, Stanstead (now Brome) County. Elder Pratt said that his sermon was "upon the gathering of Israel and more revelations and miracles, the 29th and 40th chapters of Isaiah and the two sticks." Orson spent but one day in Lower Canada, and then returned to the state of Vermont (TWP 16).

■  HATLEY—**Home of Jeremiah and Sarah Sturdevant Leavitt, Progenitors of Gov. Michael O. Leavitt of Utah**

The village of **Hatley, Hatley Township, Stanstead County** is located four miles east of the south end of **Lac Massawippi** on Highway 208.

**Sarah Sturdevant** was married to **Jeremiah Leavitt II** on Mar. 6, 1817, at her father's house in the town of Barton, Orleans County, VT. The young couple moved to Hatley, Lower Canada, that same year. One night Sarah experienced an unusual succession of heavenly lights, which appeared in her room. She did not know the interpretation of the lights until she heard the gospel preached to her. Sarah then discerned that "the last light was the gospel preached by the angel flying through the midst of heaven, and it was the same year and the same season of the year, and I don't know but the same day that the Lord brought the glad news of salvation to Joseph Smith" (WV 26–28).

One of her husband's sisters confided to Sarah that she had heard the gospel preached by a Mormon and had believed it and was baptized. As she rehearsed to Sarah the vision of Joseph Smith and the coming of the angel Moroni, Sarah declared, "I considered it of more importance than anything I had ever heard before, for it brought back the ancient order of things and laid a foundation that could be built upon that was permanent; a foundation made by Him that laid the foundation of the earth, even the Almighty God" (WV 30). We know that **Elder Hazen Aldrich** was preaching in Hatley and vicinity in 1836. Perhaps he or an associate was the bearer of the word that touched Jeremiah's sister. Elder Aldrich stated: "From Underhill (Chittenden County, Vermont) I went into the province of Lower Canada [now Quebec]; took me up a circuit in the towns of Stanstead, Stanstead County, Hatley, Compton, Compton County, and Bamston [Barnston], Province of Quebec, where I spent the most of my time for three months. School houses were opened in almost every district and I improved the time as the Lord gave me strength. I baptized eleven persons and many more were searching the Scriptures to see if the things preached were so. I left them in the care of Elder Winslow Farr to carry on the work, for I believe that it has just begun" (JH Oct. 10, 1836).

The Leavitt family affirms that a still later contact with Mormonism occurred when a man who had attended a gathering of the Mormons came into town with copies of the **Book of Mormon** and Parley P. Pratt's, *A Voice of Warning.* He allowed the Leavitt family to take them and examine their content. Sarah's husband,

Jeremiah II, explained, "We believed them without preaching." Many of the extended Leavitt family were converted. They left Hatley on July 20, 1837, to gather with the Saints in Kirtland and other locations (ORE 3–14).

It is of historical interest to note that **Governor Michael O. Leavitt** of Utah is a fifth-generation descendant of these early Canadian Saints, Sarah and Jeremiah Leavitt II, who emigrated to Utah during the early pioneer period (AF, Leavitt).

*Utah Governor Michael O. Leavitt (courtesy of Gov. Leavitt)*

■ FREDERICTON, NEW BRUNSWICK

**Fredericton,** the capital of **New Brunswick,** is situated on a bend of the **St. Johns River.** Trans-Canada Highway 2 runs through Fredericton.

**Elders Jesse W. Crosby** and **Benjamin Brown** crossed from Quebec into New Brunswick in 1844. Elder Crosby stated, "we found ourselves in a country where no Latter-day Saint had ever journeyed and where the fulness of the gospel had never been heard." Elder Crosby further related, "Our labors were hard—yet the Lord was with us, and 'confirmed the word with signs following,' so that notwithstanding opposition from rulers, and threats—yea, violence from mobs, we were enabled to plant the standard of truth in New Brunswick." Elder Brown was beaten unmercifully by a mob of some 11 men. He later recorded, "Some

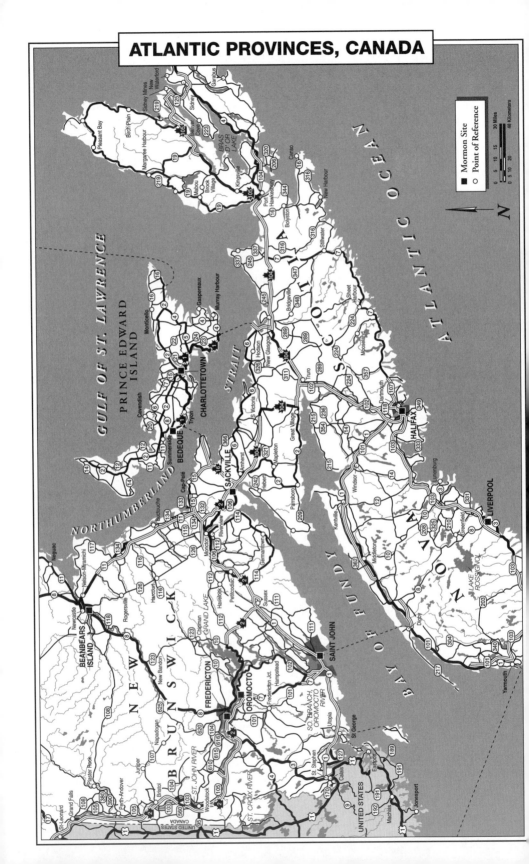

# ATLANTIC PROVINCES, CANADA

of them then threw me down, and jumped upon me with their knees until they broke several of my ribs. All this while I had been calling out loudly, whenever they did not stop my mouth." Both elders were attacked by a mob, which was completely out of control and bent on their literal destruction. Elder Brown recalled their threat to take the two missionaries to "the middle of the St. John's river, and after tying stones to our feet, sink us both." Nevertheless, laboring into the late fall of 1844, the elders converted 47 people to the new covenant and organized them into **two branches,** which were both in the county of York above Fredericton (JH Nov. 19, 1844; HCC 53–57).

- **SOUTH BRANCH OF THE OROMOCTO RIVER—Home of Jason Mack, Brother of Lucy Mack Smith**

The **South Branch** of the **Oromocto River** lies SW of the community of **Oromocto.** Oromocto is nine miles SE of Fredricton.

**Jason Mack,** brother of **Lucy Mack Smith,** fought in the Revolutionary War, and at one juncture went to sea on a privateering expedition with his father, **Solomon,** and brother **Stephen Mack.** At the conclusion of hostilities, Jason and his father "freighted a vessel" for Liverpool, NS, 75 miles SW of Halifax. Later, Solomon and Jason returned to Liverpool to collect "a heavy debt that had been due [Solomon] for a long time," and stayed for an extended period. Thus Jason was familiar with the area of the Canadian Maritime Provinces (HJS 6–7, 9–11).

Jason had become a preacher of the gospel at age 20—no denomination was specified by Lucy (HJS 9). While Lucy and Joseph Smith Sr. were living on the Tunbridge, VT, farm, Jason came and dropped off a "friendless orphan whom he had adopted" by the name of **William Smith.** In six months Jason was back, picked up the boy, and took him to New Brunswick. Here Jason had "gathered together some thirty families on a tract of land which he had purchased for the purpose of assisting poor persons to the means of sustaining themselves." Whatever they raised for sale was marketed for them by Jason. He owned a schooner and would take their produce to Liverpool, NS. The possible site of this communitarian endeavor can perhaps be identified from a letter which Jason sent 20 years later to his brother Solomon Jr. The correspondence was sent from the "South Branch of Ormucto [Oromocto], Province of New Brunswick," and dated June 30, 1835. (It is not known for certain whether this was the site where Jason and the associated families were working together or if their society was still intact at that late juncture.) Lucy further recalled, "The next intelligence we received concerning Jason, after his letter to Brother Solomon, was that he, his wife, and oldest son were dead, and this concludes my account of my brother Jason" (HJS 40–42).

■ **SAINT JOHN, NEW BRUNSWICK—Elder Lyman E. Johnson's Field of Labor**

**Saint John** is situated on the south-central coast of New Brunswick. In 1631 Charles de la Tour built a fortified trading post here. Several thousand British Loyalists from the United States founded Canada's first incorporated city at this location in 1783. Highway 1 is a major access route to the city.

Elder Lyman E. Johnson wrote to Oliver Cowdery from Saco, ME, on June 26, 1836, explaining that he had visited Saint John and from here preached in various directions "to crowded assemblies" (M&A 2:352).

■ **BEAUBEARS ISLAND—Home of the Joseph Merrill Family**

**Beaubears Island** is situated at the junction of the **Northwest Miramichi River** and the **Southwest Miramichi River,** 1.2 miles directly south of **Newcastle,** near Highway 8, and immediately west of **Nelson-Miramichi.** The island is "¼ miles in length [and] half a mile wide" (JWW 3:469).

On Apr. 22, 1848, Wilford Woodruff was appointed by President Brigham Young over the work of the ministry in the "Eastern states, Canada, New Brunswick, Nova Scotia and adjacent islands" (JH Apr. 22, 1848). **Woodruff** journeyed from Fredericton to Miramichi by stage and then crossed to Beaubears Island on a ferryboat. Arriving at the home of **Joseph** and **Ann Agnes Russell** on July 21, 1849. Elder Woodruff said, "I was thankful to strike Hands with & see a latter Day Saint after travelling two weeks without seeing any Saints. Brother Russell was a ship builder and had owned the whole island for eleven years. During that time he had built twenty-three ships with an average weight of 650 tons each" (JWW 3:469–70). Wilford estimated Brother Russell's "low rate" worth to be $30,000 in addition to three ships on hand.

Joseph Russell was the presiding elder over a small branch on the island. Russell had a chapel in his own home and Elder Woodruff commented, "I was much edifyed with his teachings & pleased with the order He had carried out in his meetings & family circle." Woodruff had an opportunity to preach to the Saints and, while on the island, to **baptize Archibald Russell** the son of Joseph Russell. Elder Woodruff stated, "I received great kindness from Brother & Sister Russell who are Israelites indeed & full of faith & good works. Our hearts were knit together and I felt it good to be under their roof & in their society. I shall long remember my visit with them" (JWW 3:470–72).

■ SACKVILLE—**Birthplace of Elder Marriner Wood Merrill**

**Sackville** is located in SE New Brunswick, 24 miles SE of **Moncton,** on Trans-Canada Highway 2.

*Marriner Wood Merrill, Apostle*

**Apostle Marriner Wood Merrill** was born in Sackville, Westmoreland County, on Sept. 25, 1832, the son of **Nathan Merrill** and **Sarah Ann Reynolds.** When but nine years of age Marriner experienced a **vision** in which he saw Joseph Smith and Brigham Young. He also witnessed the exodus of the Saints from Nauvoo to the Salt Lake Valley. In the vision, he "comprehended the doctrines and principles as they had been revealed," and a voice declared their truthfulness (BiE 1:156). Marriner was cautioned to keep to himself what he had seen. Unbeknownst to the family, his mother, Sarah Ann, had secretly joined the Church in 1836. It was only at age 18 that Marriner learned of his mother's conversion, which announcement was made following the death of his father Nathan. Elder Lyman E. Johnson, who served as a missionary in New Brunswick, represented the 19 members of the Sackville Branch at a conference of the Church held in Newry, Oxford County, ME, Aug. 12–14, 1836 (M&A 2:381–82). There was obviously a Church presence in Sackville at the time Sarah Ann Merrill secretly joined the Saints in 1836.

Although taught the gospel by a native elder, it was not until **Elders John Skerry** and **Jesse W. Crosby** came into the neighborhood that Marriner became a member of the Church. He was baptized by Elder Skerry on Apr. 3, 1852. Years later, on Oct. 7, 1889, **President**

**Wilford Woodruff** ordained Marriner W. Merrill a member of the Quorum of the Twelve Apostles in Salt Lake City. Elder Merrill presided over the Logan Temple as its first president (May 21, 1884 to Feb. 6, 1906). He died at Richmond, UT, on Feb. 6, 1906 (BiE 1:156–61; 3:764; CN May 20, 1978; DNCA 1995–96:53).

■ PRINCE EDWARD ISLAND—**The Bedeque Branch**

**Bedeque** is a small community in the Atlantic Province of **Prince Edward Island,** 5 miles SE of **Summerside** on Highway 10. The island is the **smallest Canadian province.**

    **Elders Wilford Woodruff** and **Joseph Russell** left the port of Shediac, NB, by packet boat for Prince Edward Island on July 30, 1849. Arriving in Bedeque Harbor they hired a man to drive them to the home of **Brother William Maxfield** in Bedeque. Always having an eye out for fishing, Elder Woodruff said that on the 31st he, "went to A stream near by and caught about a dozen salt water trout." Wilford also declared, "I found Prince Edwards Island A beautiful farming country" (JWW 3:473). Perchance the writer of a later period, Lucy Maud Montgomery, a native of the island and author of *Anne of Green Gables* (set in Cavendish, PEI), described the environs best when she said: "You never know what peace is until you walk on the shores or in the fields or along the winding red roads . . . on a summer twilight when the dew is falling and the old, old stars are peeping out and the sea keeps its nightly tryst with the little land it loves. You find your soul then" (CN July 10, 1993, p. 8).

    On the afternoon of July 31, the elders went to the home of **Brother John Peter Pickets** and met with the "22 members & 4 Priests" in the **Bedeque Branch.** Elder John Skerry had formed the first branch at Bedeque in Nov. 1845, consisting of one Elder, one Priest, and 10 members (JH Mar 2, 1846). Elder Woodruff was told of an additional four members who were residing in **Charlottetown,** the provincial capital to the east. The following day Elder Woodruff reorganized the Bedeque Branch with William Maxfield as presiding elder. Much useful instruction was given on emigration and the location of the pioneers in the Salt Lake Valley by Elder Woodruff (JWW 3:473).

    On Aug. 2, 1849, Elders Woodruff and Russell set out on the packet boat for their return to Shediac, NB. Elder Woodruff gave the parting hand to Elder Russell on Aug. 5. Before their separation, Elder Russell, the shipbuilder from Beaubears Island, gave Elder Woodruff a new set of clothes, paid his expenses, gave him money to help him home, and then deposited $1500 in his hands with which to help the Saints in their new home in the Salt Lake Valley. Wilford prayed, "May the Lord bless him & reward him fourfold" (JWW 3:474–75; WW 338).

■ HALIFAX BRANCH, NOVA SCOTIA

**Halifax,** the provincial capital, is located on the south-central coast of **Nova Scotia.** It is the **oldest British town** on the Canadian mainland. Settlement was begun here in July 1749 by **Colonel Edward Cornwallis.** Halifax has a huge sheltered bay that serves as its harbor. It was originally founded for strategic reasons, and still maintains an important Canadian naval base along with its vast commercial interests.

Among the very **first missionaries** to proselyte in Nova Scotia were **Elders Lyman E. Johnson** and **John Heriot** in 1832 (MS 27:102). The scope of their labors is ill-defined at present.

A **branch** of the Church was organized in Halifax on Nov. 18, 1843, consisting of 16 members. At the organizational meeting **Elder John Dixon** was appointed president and **Elder Edward Cooke** as clerk. During that meeting **John Skerry** was ordained an elder and **William Gumb** a deacon (JH Nov. 18, 1843).

Halifax was the gathering place for an area conference on Dec. 10, 1845. Elder John Skerry presided at the conference, and John Gumb served as clerk. Elder Skerry represented the 16 members of the Halifax Branch, **Priest John Whiston** represented the six members and one priest in the **Preston Branch. Elder Middlemass** reported for the eight members from the **Pope's Harbor Branch,** and also for the two members in the **Sheet Harbor Branch.** Elder Skerry also represented the 12 members of the **Bedeque Branch, PEI,** and the three members in **Onslow, Colchester County, NS.** The minutes of the conference were forwarded to **Elder Samuel Brannan** of New York City "with a letter for counsel" (HCM Nov. 18, 1843; Dec. 10, 1845).

It has been estimated that during the period of intensive missionary activity between 1832 and 1846 some 1,500 to 2,000 Canadian converts were brought into the Church—a bountiful harvest of valued contributors to the growth of the Kingdom of God on earth (UC 75).

# ABOUT THE GENERAL EDITOR

**Dr. LaMar C. Berrett** is a professor emeritus of Church History and Doctrine at Brigham Young University. He was born and reared in Riverton, UT, and served as a rifleman and platoon runner in the Second Infantry Division of the United States Army during World War II. While serving, Dr. Berrett spent 110 "combat days" in Belgium, Germany, and Czechoslovakia during the famous "Battle of the Bulge." He later served a mission in the Southern states where he served as a counselor to the mission president, and has since served in many positions in the Church including stake clerk, high councilor, bishop's counselor, and bishop. He was a member of the Church Historical Arts and Sites subcommittee for three years, and was the president of his family genealogical organization for 25 years.

Dr. Berrett received a bachelor's degree in business from the University of Utah, and a master's degree in Church history and philosophy, and a doctorate in educational administration from BYU. Following nine years as a seminary teacher, Dr. Berrett joined the BYU faculty, teaching at the university for 29 years and serving as the chair of the Church History Department for nine years before his retirement in 1991.

Over fifty percent of the text of *Sacred Places* was written by Dr. Berrett, and he has overseen the production of all of the maps included in the series and is responsible for all photographs unless otherwise noted.

Dr. Berrett has researched, written, and directed many TV and video productions for use in the classroom. He is the author of several books, including the much acclaimed *Discovering the World of the Bible.* He conducted a comprehensive aerial photography project in 1978, which involved infrared photography of significant Church history sites from New Hampshire to Salt Lake City. Dr. Berrett has also conducted numerous Church history travel tours and has hosted over 150 tours worldwide.

A lifetime of researching the history of The Church of

Jesus Christ of Latter-day Saints has been to Dr. Berrett a "soul-satisfying labor of love."

Dr. Berrett and his wife, the former Darlene Hamilton, reside in Orem, UT. The couple have nine children.

# ABOUT THE AUTHORS

৵

**Dr. Donald Q. Cannon** is a professor of Church History and Doctrine at Brigham Young University. He holds degrees from the University of Utah and Clark University. Dr. Cannon joined the BYU faculty in 1973, after having taught history at the University of Southern Maine. He has served as the Associate Dean of Religious Education in addition to other assignments while at BYU. An accomplished author and researcher, Dr. Cannon is married to the former JoAnn McGinnis, and the couple are the parents of six children.

**Dr. A. Gary Anderson** was an associate professor of Church History and Doctrine at Brigham Young University. He held degrees from both the University of Utah and BYU. Dr. Anderson had worked as a seminary and institute teacher, and as an institute director prior to his faculty appointment at BYU. He was married to the former Annette Dean, with whom he had nine children. After a bout with cancer, Dr. Anderson died in 1995.

**Dr. Larry E. Dahl** is a professor of Church History and Doctrine at Brigham Young University. Dr. Dahl began his career as a public school teacher after receiving a degree from the University of Alberta. He then worked in a number capacities for the Church Educational System and the Melchizedek Priesthood Department's curriculum office. After taking degrees in religious education and educational administration from BYU, he joined the BYU faculty. He has since served as the chair of the Department of Church History and Doctrine and as the Associate Dean of Religious Education. He has authored numerous articles and edited several books. Dr. Dahl is married to the former Roberta Erickson, and the couple are the parents of nine children.

**Dr. Larry C. Porter** is a professor of Church History and Doctrine at Brigham Young University. He has degrees from both Utah State University and BYU. Dr. Porter spent 11 years with the Church Educational System before joining the faculty at BYU. He has served as chair of the Church History and Doctrine

Department and as the director of the Church history area of the BYU Religious Studies Center. He, too, is an accomplished author. He was appointed as the Richard L. Evans Professor of Religious Understanding at BYU in 1999. Dr. Porter is married to the former LaDawn Thain, with whom he has nine children.

# ABBREVIATIONS USED IN PHOTO CAPTIONS

ﾞ❧

LDSCA    Archives Division, Church Historical Department, The Church of Jesus Christ of Latter-day Saints, Salt Lake City, UT

RLDSLA   Library-Archives and Museum, Reorganized Church of Jesus Christ of Latter Day Saints, World Headquarters, Independence, MO

USHS     Utah State Historical Society, Salt Lake City, UT

# BIBLIOGRAPHY

ﾞ❧

AAB      Whitmer, David. *An Address to All Believers in Christ.* Richmond, MO: n.p., 1887.

ABM      Van Wagoner, Richard S., and Steven C. Walker. *A Book of Mormons.* Salt Lake City: Signature Books, 1986.

AF       Ancestral File. LDS Family and Local History Library, Salt Lake City.

AHIH     Hinckley, Lorin A. *Azra Erastus Hinckley and Ira Nathanial Hinckley, Descendents and Ancestors.* Salt Lake City: n.p., 1979.

ANK      Knight, Newel. "Newel Knight's Journal." In *Scraps of Biography.* Salt Lake City: Juvenile Instructor Office, 1883. *Scraps of Biography* was reprinted as part of the 4-vols.-in-1 publication *Classical Experiences and Adventures.* Salt Lake City: Bookcraft, 1969.

APPP     Pratt, Parley P. *Autobiography of Parley Parker Pratt.* 3d. ed. Salt Lake City: Deseret Book Co., 1938.

AWH        Hyde, William. *The Private Journal of William Hyde.* Special Collections, Harold B. Lee Library Brigham, Young University, Provo, UT.

BiE        Jenson, Andrew, comp. *Biographical Encyclopedia.* 4 vols. Salt Lake City: Andrew Jenson History Co., 1901–36; Salt Lake City: Western Epics, 1971.

BoK        Pusey, Merlo J. *Builders of the Kingdom, George A. Smith, John Henry Smith, George Albert Smith.* Provo, UT: Brigham Young University Press, 1981.

BOM        Bushman, Richard L. *Joseph Smith and the Beginnings of Mormonism.* Urbana: University of Illinois Press, 1984.

BYAM       Arrington, Leonard J. *Brigham Young: American Moses.* New York: Alfred A. Knopf, 1985.

BYUS       *Brigham Young University Studies.* Published quarterly at Brigham Young University, Provo, UT.

CHC        Roberts, Brigham H. *A Comprehensive History of The Church of Jesus Christ of Latter-day Saints.* 6 vols. Salt Lake City: The Church of Jesus Christ of Latter-day Saints, 1930.

CHFT       *Church History in the Fulness of Times* [Church Educational System Manual]. Salt Lake City: The Church of Jesus Christ of Latter-day Saints, 1989.

CN         *Church News.* Salt Lake City: The Church of Jesus Christ of Latter-day Saints, 1936–.

CoCo       Snow, Bert. "A Monumental Task." *Barre (Vermont) Country Courier,* 10 Mar. 1989.

CTP        Prete, Carma T. Interview by Larry C. Porter. Kingston, ON, Canada.

DCE        Brewster, Hoyt W. *Doctrine and Covenants Encyclopedia.* Salt Lake City: Bookcraft, 1988.

DHS        Stout, Hosea. *Diary of Hosea Stout,* vol. 1. 1st ed. Ed. Juanita Brooks. Salt Lake City: University of Utah Press, 1964.

DN         *Salt Lake City Deseret News,* 1850–.

DNCA       *Deseret News Church Almanac.* Published biannually in Salt Lake City by the Deseret News in cooperation with the LDS Church Historical Department, 1974–.

DOB        Perley, Sidney. *Dwellings of Boxford.* Salem, MA: Essex Institute, 1893.

EAR        Backman, Milton V. *Eyewitness Accounts of the Restoration.* Salt Lake City: Deseret Book Co., 1986.

ECH      Smith, Joseph Fielding. *Essentials in Church History*, 13th ed. Salt Lake City: Deseret News Press, 1953.

EDH      Hinckley, Eldon H. Interview by Larry C. Porter. American Fork, UT.

EJ      *Elder's Journal of the Church of Latter Day Saints.* Kirtland, OH, Oct.–Dec. 1837; Far West, MO, July–Aug. 1838.

EMS      *Evening & Morning Star.* Published in Independence, MO, June 1832–July 1833; Kirtland, OH, Dec. 1833–Sept. 1834.

EnH      Jenson, Andrew. *Encyclopedic History of The Church of Jesus Christ of Latter-day Saints.* Salt Lake City: Deseret News Publishing Co., 1941.

EnM      Ludlow, Daniel H., ed. *Encyclopedia of Mormonism.* 5 vols. New York: Macmillan Publishing Co., 1992.

ENS      *Ensign.* Published monthly by The Church of Jesus Christ of Latter-day Saints, Salt Lake City, 1971–.

ER      *Salem (Mass.) Essex Register.*

ES      Larson, Andrew Karl. *Erastus Snow: The Life of a Missionary and Pioneer for the Early Mormon Church.* Salt Lake City: University of Utah Press, 1971.

ETB      Dew, Sheri L. *Ezra Taft Benson: A Biography.* Salt Lake City: Deseret Book Co., 1987.

FOP      Quincy, Josiah. *Figures of the Past From the Leaves of Old Journals.* Boston: Boston Brothers, 1883.

FWR      *Far West Record: Minutes of The Church of Jesus Christ of Latter-day Saints, 1830–1844.* Eds. Donald Q. Cannon and Lyndon W. Cook. Salt Lake City: Deseret Book Co., 1983.

GMH      Claude, William, and Eloise Richards Anderson. *Guide Book to Mormon History Travel.* Provo, UT: Bushman Press, 1991.

HC      Smith, Joseph, Jr. *History of The Church of Jesus Christ of Latter-day Saints.* 7 vols. Ed. B. H. Roberts. 2d rev. ed. Salt Lake City: Deseret Book Co., 1951.

HCC      Tagg, Melvin S. "A History of The Church of Jesus Christ of Latter-day Saints in Canada, 1830–1963." Ph.D. diss., Brigham Young University, 1963.

HCKM      Kimball, Stanley B. *Heber C. Kimball: Mormon Patriarch and Pioneer.* Urbana: University of Illinois Press, 1981.

HCM      Jenson, Andrew, comp. "History of the Canadian Mission," LDS Church Archives, Salt Lake City, UT.

HeR     Backman, Milton V., Jr. *The Heavens Resound: A History of the Latter-day Saints in Ohio, 1830–1838.* Salt Lake City: Deseret Book Co., 1983.

HIB     Young, S. Dilworth. *Here Is Brigham . . .* Salt Lake City: Bookcraft, 1964.

HiB     Perley, Sidney. *The History of Boxford, Essex County, Massachusetts.* Boxford, MA: The author, 1880.

HiR     *The Historical Record.* (Periodical published monthly in Salt Lake City by Andrew Jenson, Assistant Church Historian, 1882–90.) Vols. 5–8 published in *Church Encyclopedia.* Book 1. Salt Lake City: Andrew Jenson, 1889.

HJ      Judd, Henry. Interview by Larry C. Porter. Delta, Leeds-Greenville Co., ON, Canada.

HJS     Smith, Lucy Mack. *History of Joseph Smith by His Mother, Lucy Mack Smith.* Salt Lake City: Bookcraft, 1958.

HJWI    Willey, Jeremiah. "History of Jeremiah Willey, 1804–1868." Holograph. LDS Church Archives, Salt Lake City, UT.

HOU     Neff, Andrew L. *History of Utah, 1847–1869.* Ed. Leland Hargrave Creer. Salt Lake City: Deseret News Press, 1940.

HTZ     Hafen, Le Roy Reuben, and Ann W. Hafen. *Handcarts to Zion.* Vol. 14 of *Far West and Rockies Series.* Glendale, CA: The Arthur H. Clark Co., 1960.

HWP     Barnouw, Erik. *House with a Past.* Montpelier, VT: Vermont Historical Society, 1992.

InD     Noall, Claire A. W. *Intimate Disciple: A Portrait of Willard Richards, Apostle to Joseph Smith, Cousin of Brigham Young.* Salt Lake City: University of Utah Press, 1957.

JDW     Wood, Daniel. Journal of Daniel Wood, vol. 1. LDS Church Archives, Salt Lake City, UT.

JH      "Journal History of The Church of Jesus Christ of Latter-day Saints." Manuscript. LDS Church Archives, Salt Lake City, UT.

JI      *Juvenile Instructor.* (Variant title of *The Instructor.*) Published bi-weekly, monthly. Salt Lake City: Deseret Sunday School Union, 1866–1929.

JOP     Pratt, Orson. Journal. LDS Church Archives, Salt Lake City, UT.

JSN     Anderson, Richard L. *Joseph Smith's New England Heritage.* Salt Lake City: Deseret Book Co., 1971.

JWW     Woodruff, Willford. *Wilford Woodruff's Journal, 1833–1898.* 9 vols. Ed. Scott G. Kenney. Midvale, UT: Signature Books, 1983.

KEQR     Backman, Milton V., Jr., and Lyndon W. Cook, eds. *Kirtland Elders' Quorum Record 1836–1841.* Provo, UT: Grandin Book Company, 1985.

LAG     Hughes, Delila Gardner. *Life of Archibald Gardner.* N.p.: Alpine Publishing Co., 1939.

LAP     Evans, John Henry. *Joseph Smith: An American Prophet.* Salt Lake City: Deseret Book Co., 1989.

LHCK     Whitney, Orson F. *Life of Heber C. Kimball.* 3d ed. Salt Lake City: Bookcraft, 1967.

LJT     Roberts, B. H. *The Life of John Taylor, Third President of The Church of Jesus Christ of Latter-day Saints.* Salt Lake City: Bookcraft, 1963.

M&A     *Messenger and Advocate.* Kirtland, OH: The Church of Jesus Christ of Latter-day Saints, 1834–37.

MAR     Lichfield, Walter C. "Thomas B. Marsh, Physician to the Church." Master's thesis, Brigham Young University, 1956.

MHBY     Young, Brigham. *Manuscript History of Brigham Young.* Ed. Elden Jay Watson. Vol. 1801–1844, Salt Lake City: Smith Secretarial Services, 1968. Vol. 1846–1847, Salt Lake City: E. J. Watson, 1971.

MNE     Williams, Richard Shelton. "The Missionary Movements of the Latter-day Saint Church in New England, 1830–1850." Master's thesis, Brigham Young University, 1969.

MOC     Black, Susan Easton, comp. *Membership of The Church of Jesus Christ of Latter-day Saints, 1830–1848.* 50 vols. (Alphabetized by member name). Provo, UT: Brigham Young University, Religious Studies Center, 1984–88.

MoP     McGavin, Elmer Cecil. *The Mormon Pioneers.* Salt Lake City: Stevens & Wallis, 1947.

MoS     Whitney, Orson F. *The Making of a State: A School History of Utah.* Salt Lake City: Deseret News, 1908.

MS     *Millennial Star.* Liverpool: The Church of Jesus Christ of Latter-day Saints, 1840–1970.

MTVU     Burton, Alma P. *The Mormon Trail from Vermont to Utah.* Salt Lake City: Deseret Book Co., 1966.

NAU     Godfrey, Kenneth W. "Causes of Mormon/Non-

|          | Mormon Conflict in Hancock County, Illinois, 1839–1846." Ph.D. diss., Brigham Young University, 1967. |
|----------|----------------------------------------------------------------------------------------------------------|
| NEW      | Porter, Larry C. "A Study of the Origins of The Church of Jesus Christ of Latter-day Saints in the States of New York and Pennsylvania, 1816–1831." Ph.D. diss., Brigham Young University, 1971. |
| OBT      | O'Brien, Robert. *On the Beginnings of Tunbridge.* [Montpelier, VT?]: n.p., [1961?]. |
| OIC      | Gunn, Stanley R. *Oliver Cowdery: Second Elder and Scribe.* Salt Lake City: Bookcraft, 1962. |
| OMN      | Holzapfel, Richard N., and T. Jeffrey Cottle. *Old Mormon Nauvoo, 1839–1846.* Provo, UT: Grandin Book, 1990. |
| OPR      | Schindler, Harold. *Orrin Porter Rockwell: Man of God, Son of Thunder.* Salt Lake City: University of Utah Press, 1966. |
| OrH      | Barron, Howard H. *Orson Hyde: Missionary, Apostle, Colonizer.* Bountiful, UT: Horizon Publishers, 1977. |
| PaD      | Smith, Joseph F. *Proceedings at the Dedication of the Joseph Smith Memorial Monument.* Salt Lake City: The Church of Jesus Christ of Latter-day Saints, 1906. |
| PION     | Mika, Nick, and Helma Mika. *Places in Ontario.* Belleville, ON: Mika Publishing Co., 1977. |
| PJE      | Porter, Larry C., and Susan Easton Black, eds. *The Prophet Joseph: Essays on the Life and Mission of Joseph Smith.* Salt Lake City: Deseret Book Co., 1988. |
| PWJS     | Smith, Joseph. *The Personal Writings of Joseph Smith.* Ed. Dean C. Jessee. Salt Lake City: Deseret Book Co., 1984. |
| ReS      | Cannon, Donald Q., ed. *Regional Studies in Latter-day Saint Church History, New England.* Provo, UT: Department of Church History and Doctrine, Brigham Young University, 1988. |
| ReSNY    | Porter, Larry C., Milton V. Backman, and Susan Easton Black, eds. *Regional Studies in Latter-day Saint Church History, New York.* Provo, UT: Department of Church History and Doctrine, Brigham Young University, 1992. |
| RLDS     | Littlefield, Lyman Omer. *Reminiscences of Latter-day Saints.* Logan, UT: The Utah Journal Co., 1888. |
| RoJS     | Smith, John. "John Smith's 1839 Recollections." In *Joseph Smith's New England Heritage,* Richard L. Anderson. Salt Lake City: Deseret Book Co., 1971. |

RPJS    Cook, Lyndon W. *The Revelations of the Prophet Joseph Smith: A Historical and Biographical Commentary of the Doctrine and Covenants.* Provo, UT: Seventy's Mission Bookstore, 1981.

SA    *Scientific American.* New York: Scientific American, Inc.

SB    Luce, W. Ray. "Samuel Brannan: Speculator in Mexican Lands." Master's thesis, Brigham Young University, 1968.

SiS    Millet, Robert L., and Kent Jackson, eds. *Studies in Scripture: Vol. 1, The Doctrine and Covenants.* Sandy, UT: Randall Book Co., 1984.

SLD    Allen, James B., and Glen M. Leonard. *The Story of the Latter-day Saints.* 2nd ed., rev., enl. Salt Lake City: Deseret Book Co., 1992.

STR    Sharon (Vermont) Town Land Records. Town Office, Sharon, VT.

T&S    *Nauvoo (Illinois) Times and Seasons.* Published monthly, 1839–46.

TAMF    Hartley, William. *They Are My Friends: A History of the Joseph Knight Family, 1825–1850.* Provo, UT: Grandin Book Co., 1986.

TFBR    *[Tolman] Family Book of Remembrance and Genealogy with Allied Lines.* N.p.: n.p., Dec. 1952.

TFo    Holmes, Reed M. *The Forerunners.* Independence, MO: Herald Publishing House, 1981.

TGCM    Hedengren, Russell, and Brant Russell, eds. *The Great Canadian Mission, A Jubilee History.* Brampton, ON: The Canadian Mission, [1969?].

ThC    *The Contributor.* Published monthly. Salt Lake City: The Contributor Co., 1879–96.

ThP    *The Prophet.* New York City: Issued by a society of the Saints, 1844–45.

TMH    Lundwall, N. B. *Temples of the Most High.* 8th ed. Salt Lake City: Bookcraft, 1952.

TrG    Oscarson, R. Don. *The Travelers Guide to Historic Mormon America.* Salt Lake City: Bookcraft, 1965.

TTR    Tunbridge (Vermont) Town Records. Land Records (Deeds, court proceedings, etc.). Acquired by Lamar Garrard, Department of Church History and Doctrine, Brigham Young University.

TWP    Bloxham, Ben V., James R. Moss, and Larry C. Porter,

eds. *Truth Will Prevail: The Rise of The Church of Jesus Christ of Latter-day Saints in the British Isles, 1837–1987.* Cambridge: The Church of Jesus Christ of Latter-day Saints, 1987.

UC Bennett, Richard E. "A Study of The Church of Jesus Christ of Latter-day Saints in Upper Canada, 1830–1850." Master's thesis, Brigham Young University, 1975.

UHE Powell, Allan Kent, ed. *Utah History Encyclopedia.* Salt Lake City: University of Utah Press, 1994.

UHQ *Utah Historical Quarterly.* Published in Salt Lake City by the Board of Control, Utah Historical Society, Jan. 1928–.

WBE *World Book Encyclopedia.* 1986 ed. s.v. "Vermont, The State of."

WBM Nibley, Preston. *The Witnesses of the Book of Mormon.* Salt Lake City: Stevens and Wallis, 1946.

WL Cook, Lyndon W. *William Law.* Orem, UT: Grandin Book Co., 1994.

WV Godfrey, Kenneth W., Audrey M. Godfrey, and Jill Mulvay Derr, eds. *Women's Voices: An Untold History of the Latter-day Saints, 1830–1900.* Salt Lake City: Deseret Book Co., 1982.

WW Woodruff, Wilford. *Wilford Woodruff, Fourth President of The Church of Jesus Christ of Latter-Day Saints.* Prepared for publication by Mathias F. Cowley. Salt Lake City: Bookcraft, 1964.

ZSCF Prete, Roy A., ed. *Zion Shall Come Forth: A History of the Ottawa Ontario Stake.* Kingston, ON: Digigraphics Inc., 1996.

# INDEX

ৰ

Note: Italicized page numbers indicate photographs or illustrations, bold faced page numbers incicate maps.